A Lifetime at War

G.L. EWELL

A Lifetime at War

Life after Being Severely Wounded
in Combat: Never-Ending Dung

GORDON L. EWELL

Order this book online at www.trafford.com
or email orders@trafford.com

Most Trafford titles are also available at major online book retailers.

Printed in the United States of America.

ISBN: 978-1-4669-3266-1 (sc)
ISBN: 978-1-4669-4624-8 (hc)
ISBN: 978-1-4669-4623-1 (e)

Library of Congress Control Number: 2012911785

Trafford rev. 11/09/2013

 www.trafford.com

North America & international
toll-free: 1 888 232 4444 (USA & Canada)
fax: 812 355 4082

To Jerral and all my brothers and sisters
who are fighting every day to win their own
war after the war.

Keep fighting the good fight.

Never give up, never say die.

Don't let the bastards win.

A man who is good enough to
shed his blood for the Country is good
enough to be given a square deal afterwards.

—President Theodore Roosevelt

A Healing Field flag display set up by Colonial Flag,
Sandy, Utah.

Preface

The tapestry of Americana is bound tightly together by the strongest of threads made from the last breath of every American soldier who died fighting for our country and with the blood that our wounded shed at war, who now gallantly press forward through life, carrying with them those scars without regret for giving their all, when upon them our Lady of Liberty called.

—Gordon Ewell

It is morning. I have been sitting in this very spot for some time now. How long, I am not sure—five or ten minutes. I wonder, but cannot seem to break away from what I am looking at. It is as if I am under some trance or under a spell. I look, squint, and try to look even harder. I want to take in every single line, every little detail, every single shade and color of what I am so deeply transfixed on. But yet, I do not want to look.

I know that I am staring, yet I am not worried that others might notice. Nor do I care. I feel sick and uneasy in my stomach, almost to the point of nausea.

But yet, I cannot seem to look away. In fact, I stare harder. Five, maybe ten minutes. I manage to break contact ever so briefly to look at a nearby clock. How has fifty minutes gone by already? How could that be so? Yet time is so irrelevant to me right now.

The image, I must get back to it. Where is he? There he is! Strange, he has not moved. He has hardly even blinked. I am back in my trancelike stare. He still hasn't moved. I want to cry for him. He looks so frail. There are scars, many of them, and burns too. He seems somewhat monster-looking but not in a scary way. Is that . . . ? Yes, it is; he only has one eye! He is looking right at me with it now. It is a cold, hard stare that feels as though he is looking right through me. I catch a glimmer of fight in it. The image is starting to become somewhat blurry. How long now? I quickly look. It has been over an hour now. I quickly look back. His eye shimmers now. He is getting tears in his eye. What to do now? I feel tears welling up inside of me. One breaks free. A single stray tear slowly streaks down his cheek. I suddenly feel one on my cheek! God, I hope no one saw it. I hurry to wipe it away. At that very precise moment, so does he. I slowly move my hand from my cheek.

I feel the urge to reach out to him now. My hand slowly stretches toward him on its own. I am unable to pull it back. I stop trying, now wanting it to go, as I notice that he is now reaching too . . . for me.

My hand hits the mirror, and reality comes crashing down upon me with the weight of a thousand horrific memories that I had tried to keep safely buried away.

My mind becomes a thunderstorm of ear-shattering clashes as blinding lightning-strike images flash through my mind. Images of me—a strong, healthy, and happy me. Me, before I left to go to war. I was a good-looking, strong, strapping man, full of pride.

I was a career soldier by trade, a warrior fighting in a foreign land, in Iraq, because I needed to protect all that I believed in. Because that was where I was ordered to go, to help bring justice to those who sought to take all that I believed in away from me and my family when they attacked my precious America!

Images I am having now of an ambush and of explosions. Memories I am having now of a thunderous, deafening explosion and a blinding flash of light. Suddenly, I recall the memory of no light or sound—nothing but total blindness and deadly silence.

Faintly, the sounds of a .50 caliber machine gun begin to get louder, and I recall blurry images starting to appear as the smoke filling the vehicle tries to escape. The memory of burning hair is so strong I think I can smell it now.

My chest feels as if it were on fire. I remember gasping for breath and the burning pain in my lungs. I grab at my chest. But wait, what is this? So does the man in the mirror!

As instantly as they arrived, the images of war are gone and replaced with the feeling of air returning to my lungs and the sound of tears being choked back.

Slowly I let my hand fall to my lap. As I sit in my wheelchair, I already know. But I allow my head to rise slowly, and I find again and stare once more at the man in the mirror. The man I had been trying so hard to recognize—*me*.

It is said that one definition of hell is when "the man you are meets the man you *could* have been."

For this severely wounded soldier, my hell began when the man I saw in the mirror remembered the man he *was*.

Come along. It's time to move on . . .

Contents

Section One

Chapter One: Meet the New You...3
Chapter Two: My Morning Routine.............................. 10
Chapter Three: Homebound....................................... 19
Chapter Four: Going Somewhere 31
Chapter Five: Get a Life.. 37
Chapter Six: It Takes a Team...................................... 47
Chapter Seven: Depression Will Find You 54
Chapter Eight: Combat-Related Post-Traumatic
      Stress Disorder (PTSD).. 63
Chapter Nine: Fight for Everything............................. 79
Chapter Ten: Lean on Me.. 85

Section Two

Poems and Poetry of the Combat Soldier

A Day from Hell 95
I May Take a Life Tonight 97
Just Another Day... 101
I Wait and Smoke.. 103
Holiday Opposites 105
The War after the War.. 107
Thoughts before Battle by Richard Hamilton 110
Soldier's Return by Richard Hamilton 111
In Your Honor by Richard Hamilton 113
Friends by Richard Hamilton 115
Portrait of a Friend by Richard Hamilton..................... 117

Section Three

Gordy-isms

Original thoughts, comments, and quotes from the postwar mind of the recovering author.

List of Illustrations

Illustrated by Gordon L. Ewell

Listed in the order they appear in the book. First is the name of the illustration, then its location in the book.

1. Engineer Castle (frontispiece and last page of chapter 2 and chapter 5)

2. My Mobility Devices (page before chapter 1)

3. Iron Cross (last page of chapter 5)

4. A Dead Man's Hand (last page of chapter 6)

5. Danger Mines (last page of chapter 7)

6. M1A1 Battle Tank (last page of chapter 9)

7. Angel Wings (last page of chapter 10)

8. Coffee Hands (first page of Gordy-isms)

9. Battle Cross (last page of book)

SECTION ONE

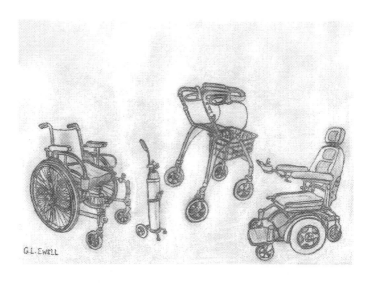

My Mobility Devices

Chapter One

Meet the New You

A new day has presented itself in all its splendor beginning with the allure and beauty of a breathtaking sunrise as its first rays of hope and promise streaked from over the mountaintops across the sky, chasing the dark of night away.

This small miracle of nature I viewed through my bedroom window from lying in bed. I did not witness it long though as I opted to close my eyes and tried to stop the pain in my head that woke me from the two hours I had been asleep. Between the pain and fatigue from being up all night long, fighting PTSD (post-traumatic stress syndrome), my war demons, my eye rolled easily back into my foggy head for two more hours. Now it's already pushing midmorning as I lay awake in bed, trying to decide if I am ready mentally to make an honest effort to try to get out of bed. I have shaken most of the cobwebs from my mind and am beginning to have rational thoughts. I know who I am, have scanned my surroundings and recognized where I am. I am home. To know this little bit of information is a real big relief. I immediately count this as the first real success, or positive thing, that has happened today. Knowing there will be many negative things as well, I have learned to start early accounting for each victory.

The rest of my reality hits me now. I am home. Back home from war in Iraq. Back home from a level one poly-trauma unit. Back home to put my life, or rather a life, together after being severely injured in the war.

A few short years ago, I would have opened my eyes and been able to see my entire bedroom in a quick glance. I would have enjoyed what I had seen and bounced out of bed to greet the day. Habit and a regimented daily routine would have had me waking without an alarm clock. I would have been up and gotten dressed in my sweats and running shoes and would have been standing in the front doorway watching the first rays of light shatter the silence of the darkness with its illuminating fingers and found joy in seeing the world react to the angelic announcement heralding the coming of the omnipotent energy, light and life-giving Mr. Sun. Upon marveling in its glorious arrival, I would be out the door for one of the joys I loved about my old routine, my morning jog. It was usually five miles, no matter the weather. I would swiftly be off down the road, enjoying the sounds of birds awaking to sing their song to others, echoing the arrival of a brand-new day. It was wonderful to jog along with a long stride and steady gait and see my sleepy little rural town awake to the new day. The same lights would already be on in the same houses. A few ladies along my route would be up and out, tending to flower gardens as a part of their morning routines. The same early commuters would be pulling out of their driveways, off to their jobs, and on the road before the rest of the regular commuters and, without fail, the same dogs awaiting my arrival to come nipping at my heels. Small trivial things I would love to have back.

The new me has only one eye with tunnel vision, no bilateral fields of view at all, and the ability to only see an area about the size of a dinner plate at one time. It takes several minutes to take in all my surroundings even though they are very familiar to me. The images are blurry at first until I remember that the new me needs to wear glasses. I fumble around for them anxiously. Upon finding my glasses and putting them on, I begin the scan of my bedroom once again. This time putting each little section of perception together like puzzle pieces inside my head to form larger images of the world that now surrounds me.

I do not have feeling in my left leg but know it is there, which brings a small bit of comfort to me (another little victory). I ache, and I am in pain. I really do not want to move at all knowing the already-intensifying pain will get worse. But move I must if I am to get to the bathroom and take my medicines, which will take the sharp edge off my pain. Not eliminate it, mind you, but make it subside enough that it is bearable and I am able to function. But first I need to tend to my leg. A residual effect of my traumatic brain injury (TBI) is that my brain and my left leg are not always on speaking terms. I must rub and massage the larger muscles in my thigh until I can get some circulation going and some kind of feeling in it so that I might have a chance of standing upright without falling flat on my face. Usually, after a few minutes of doing this, some feeling will come. If it does not, well then, I know that it will be my wheelchair I will need to get to rather than gathering in hand a support cane. This morning brings another small victory as soon my left leg begins to sting a bit when the familiar tingling returns.

Tired of the memories that have also awakened and started racing through my mind in no order, sequence, or any other format that could be labeled as organized, I finally decide I must get out of bed. I sit up and give a moment for the lightheadedness that this small action created to go away and then move my legs to the side of the bed. Again a pause, another check of my surroundings, and upon locating my support cane, I take it in hand. With the aid of the support cane and a lot of effort, mentally and physically, I shove off the bed and on my feet. Yeah! This is another small victory for me. After I have taken a moment and straightened the kinks and bends out of my body, I try to make myself stand erect and succeed.

I am up. My day has now officially started. Now, to take some steps forward, make my way to the bathroom, and see if I can make something out of it. "Good morning," I try to tell myself. Though as of yet, I have found very little pleasure in any of it.

Once in the bathroom, I immediately stop and am somewhat startled. I notice the mirror and the image staring back at me. Good hell, what an unpleasant view to wake up to. The image of the man looks horrible to me. He is—or rather, I am—thirty pounds lighter than the old me and look thin and hollow-cheeked. With a bedhead hairdo, stitches in my forehead from a fall earlier in the week, and only one eyeball—as I have yet to put my prosthetic one in its socket—I feel like Frankenstein. Or rather, like I am an anorexic, a broken and frail version of him. The morning victories get erased as I get slapped with this view of the new me. I can easily count this as my day's first mental defeat.

However, as it is a morning view I have seen for some time now, I am able to simply grunt a sound of hate for this image that I see and can proceed to take care of the morning's first priorities, the new daily routine that has replaced the early morning jogging of my past. The past, being prior to my combat tour of duty at war in Iraq. The past, prior to me being blown up six times while being a bomb hunter looking for improvised explosive devices (IEDs) on city streets and rural county roads all throughout that damned country, as well as getting shot at, ambushed, and attacked.

It does not take much for those memories to flood into my brain-damaged head. It is much harder to shove them out or shut them down so I can keep going rather than let them overcome me and mentally shut down and drown. I manage to put them in a bubble that I pretend to blow away and then wipe away a tear or two and get back to reality: me, this new me, getting ready for a brand-new day.

It used to be as easy as a quick stop at the toilet, then on to a little pick-me-up at the sink as I would wash my hands and face. I would knock what little sleep was left out of my eyes and mind as the warm water splashed upon my face, then on to taming my bedhead with a comb and brushing my teeth, followed by a good blast of mouthwash and a quick change into my jogging clothes. At most it took fifteen minutes.

Good morning, stud, and welcome to the new you. My morning ritual now will take at least an hour if I hurry some and do not get distracted at all.

At this point, relative to receiving my war injuries, I have been traveling down my recovery road now for approximately two years.

When I first returned to from Iraq and ended up at an army medical treatment facility in Fort Carson, Colorado, I was immediately diagnosed with a TBI, severe hearing loss, and loss of vision. I was further diagnosed with neurological damage, post-traumatic stress disorder (PTSD), and damage to my teeth and jaw. They had not seen a lot of TBIs at that time, and a decision was made to transfer me for treatment to the veterans' hospital in Salt Lake City, Utah. There I immediately received treatments to stabilize me medically, and they continued to further find, diagnose, and treat new injuries and wounds. Some of my injuries required referral to medical specialists outside of the veterans' hospital. This occurred immediately when it was required.

In a nutshell, I had, in direct combat with enemy forces and instruments of war, suffered severe brain damage, profound hearing loss, had a broken neck with right-side stenosis (restricted blood flow to the right side of my brain), and was found to be legally blind. I had damaged vertebrae in my lower back (L5 and L6) and had upper respiratory problems (due to the damage done to my throat and upper lungs) from inhaling the intense heat and gasses that engulfed my vehicle as the fireball of the bomb rolled over and through it. I also had a broken jaw and shattered teeth and had tremors, seizures, tics, and abnormal body movements I couldn't control; a nonworking bladder; craniofacial damage; severe pain; and PTSD.

By this time, I had received treatment in six different hospitals in three different states, had three major surgeries, and had been treated by forty-nine different primary health care specialists. I had also lived in an assisted-living facility for some six months.

I had received craniofacial reconstruction; had my left eye anatomically removed in surgery; received a cochlear implant; received extensive mental health treatment; received hyperbaric oxygen chamber treatments; had long-term hospital stays; received extensive physical therapy, speech therapy, occupational therapy, and mental health therapy; and had extensive neurological testing and treatment and medicinal treatment. There was a time when I was taking thirty-six different prescriptions at one time, morning and night. Once I had an accidental overdose and spent some time in hell, rebounding from that in an intensive care unit.

By this time, I had also been treated in an urgent-care facility or hospital emergency room over thirty-five times for severe head injuries from blackouts with falls that required ten or more stitches and often were accompanied with a concussion (that number is now up to fifty-nine). I had broken my nose three different times; nearly cut off an arm; broken two different fingers (on different occasions), which required surgery and pins to put back together; cut a finger completely off, which was saved and reattached (thanks to a very skilled hand surgeon); and been on a *straight* liquid diet, which consisted of five cans of Ensure every day—one flavor only (vanilla)—for two years (it has now been over four years).

I require a conservator to do my finances as numbers do not mean much to me. My brain just does not comprehend how to do even some basic math, which is frustrating indeed.

I require the use of a continuous pressurized air pressure (CPAP) machine, with an oxygen machine feeding it at night to breathe, as I sometimes quit breathing in my sleep.

I cannot always walk. My legs often do not want to work. In which case I am wheelchair-bound until they and my brain decide they want to communicate with each other.

When I can walk, I require a support cane in one hand, a blind man's cane in the other, and I am supposed to wear a helmet. I admit I do not always wear my helmet, which, yes, I know would have prevented some of the emergency room visits. I have also been hit by vehicles while crossing roads with my canes by people who never see the blind man. Just another part of getting used to my new world and learning the tools and techniques I need to survive in it.

You add it all together and you have the brand-new me!

One thing I did learn after twenty-four years of military service in my occupational specialties was the ability to adapt and overcome in any environment.

That is what I tell myself I must do every single day, adapt and overcome!

Chapter Two

My Morning Routine

First, I must locate my glasses and my support cane, then go drain my bladder, as most people do right after they wake up. I once stood tall before the toilet, with my manhood proudly in hand and on autopilot, without having to think about it at all. I could stand and piss a stream of urine like a man. It was a simple little task taken for granted then and only took a minute of my time. However, it is quite a different story now because of my TBI. A neurological residual effect of my brain damage is that my brain chose, among other things, to divorce my bladder. They no longer communicate. My bladder does not function on its own. A flaccid neurological bladder is the official term I believe the doctors used. All it means to me is that my bladder no longer works on its own. So what used to take me a single minute now takes five or ten, depending on how I am feeling. I require the use of a catheter to drain my bladder.

Basically, a urinary catheter is a tube that is inserted into the urethra by inserting the tube into the head of the penis on a man or through the small opening just below the clitoris and above the vagina on a woman.

You begin first by thoroughly washing your hands with soap and water. Then you must thoroughly wash around the opening you are going to insert the tubing into. As infection is a fairly high risk when using a catheter, a good cleaning is necessary to prevent getting a urinary tract infection, which, trust me, is not fun at all.

A person needs to use urinary catheters basically for one of two reasons. One, they have a condition called urinary incontinence. This simply means the bladder lacks the ability to hold urine in the bladder. You constantly leak, so to speak. The second reason is for a condition called urinary retention. This means that a person is not able to urinate, not able to drain their bladder on their own when they need to.

Urinary retention is what I suffer from. As a result of my brain injury, the message my brain sends to my bladder to open the valve either never makes it to my bladder or is not interpreted correctly when the message gets there. The result is the valve never opens. Chances are, it will never open again. Therefore, urinary catheterization is something I get to look forward to for the next forty years.

I am not an expert by any means—other than the fact that I am an expert in using a catheter. So keep that in mind as I tell you, in my own layman's terms, these are basic descriptions. I am explaining the differences, as I know them, to help in understanding why I must do what I do to drain my own bladder.

There are basically two different types of urinary catheters. These are either indwelling catheters or intermittent catheters.

Indwelling catheters are called such because they are actually placed within the bladder and remain there for a long time. A long tube with a deflated balloon attached to it is pushed up the urethra and into the bladder. Once there, a small amount of sterile water is pumped into the balloon, which expands and keeps the catheter in place as well as seals the bladder opening so urine cannot leak by it into the urethra and down your legs. Urine then flows through a long tubing system that is either attached to a bag secured to a person's lower leg or a collection bag attached to a wheelchair or attached to the side of a hospital bed. The bag must then be emptied daily and routinely cleaned. These catheters are also referred to as Foley catheters. A person using a Foley catheter is usually paralyzed, hospitalized, or otherwise unable to use and take care of other catheterization procedures on their own.

There are Texas catheters, also called condom catheters. These work the same way as a Foley catheter except that no tubing is pushed into the bladder. Basically, it is like a small condom that fits over the penis with a tube attached to it that drains the urine into a bag. The bag must then be emptied daily and routinely cleaned, just like the bag on the Foley catheter. These catheters are used only for very short periods because of the high risk for urinary tract infections, damage to the penis from the friction of the condom constantly rubbing against it (it cannot be lubricated or it would slip off the penis), and also the risk of urethral blockage because of the compression of a tightly fitted condom on the penis.

Intermittent catheters can usually be inserted by the person using them or with the aid of someone else.

Basically, when the person needs to drain their bladder, they insert a tube through the urethra, push it into the bladder, and gravity does the rest. The urine will then flow through the tube and into the toilet or a collection device, either a hard container or a bag.

This is the type of catheter I use, and thank God, I can use it rather than require one of the other types I told you about.

The tubes vary in different sizes, lengths, and hardness. The factors that determine this are the size of the opening to the urethra and the distance the tube needs to be in order to get through the urethra and into your bladder. The catheters I use are sixteen inches long and 5.3 mm in diameter. First, I clean my hands and the head of my penis. Trust me, after you get your first urinary tract infection, you are not shy about taking the time to wash your hands and penis really good.

The tubes are dry, and you would take them out of their wrapping and then would need to apply a water-based lubricant to the catheter and a small amount on the opening to the urethra—the head of my penis in my case. The instructions, which I am positive was written by someone who has never had to use a catheter, states, "Place a small amount of lubricant on about the first two inches of tubing." Believe me, the last thing you want is a dry spot of tubing grabbing the walls of your urethra as you are trying to jam a tube up a urinary tract that, by design, was meant to be a one-way road.

A small amount my ass; I lubricate the hell out of the damned things! Then firmly holding my manhood in one hand and gently pulling it straight down toward the floor, I insert the sixteen-inch catheter with my other hand. I push it about eleven inches up my urethra until it hits the opening to my bladder. Then a push through the bladder valve and about another two inches, and the flow begins. By straddling the toilet and leaning against the wall or my grab bars, I am able to drain my bladder directly into the toilet. When the flow stops, the job is finished. The catheter can then be removed. It slides right out. It can then be stuffed back into the wrapping it came out of and discarded in the trash like a woman would discard a feminine personal-hygiene product (a tampon or pad).

Technology has improved a great deal and now the catheters come prelubricated, which is very nice.

It isn't too big a deal at home. But now think of all the filthy, nasty germ-ridden bathrooms you have come across in your travels, like at convenience stores, public restrooms, Porta Potties at fairs, outdoor concerts, job sites, and some diners or truck stops. These can be scary as hell for me when I have no choice but to use one and I am thinking about personal hygiene and the risk of a bladder infection.

For this reason, I carry with me at all times what I call my man bag. It is basically a messenger bag that I have customized and tried to make it look manly by adding some military, patriotic, and biker patches and pins to it. In it I carry items I need to sterilize such germ-ridden environments to decrease my chances of getting a urinary tract infection.

I'll go into more detail about my man bag later. I am sure some people still look at me and think or say to whom they are with, "Hey, check out the dude with the purse," and chuckle. But when you have to carry around as many backup supplies for as many fake body parts as I have, it is essential, and to tell the truth, by now I could care less what people think. It is about reducing serious medical risks for me, period.

Anyway, back to my morning routine. I have basically just got my butt out of bed, into the bathroom, and have just finished draining my bladder via a catheter. Let's move on to the rest of my morning routine.

The next thing on my checklist is to brush my teeth. It is hard to feel fresh if your teeth and mouth feel and taste nasty. No big deal here. I use an electric toothbrush and have a Velcro strap I can wrap around my hand and the toothbrush if I am having trouble gripping it. It happens sometimes. Just another residual effect of my brain damage I get to deal with. Now I am in front of the bathroom mirror, seeing the same thing and thinking the same thing I do every morning: "What a monster." With morning hair, stubble on my face, and not having my fake eye in yet, I hate the way I see myself. So I mostly stare into the sink. Task done, time to shave.

I have an electric shaver, but I prefer a razor. As long as my body is not shaking uncontrollably, I use a razor. I prefer to shave close to the skin above my ears so that the processors for my hearing aid and cochlear implant fit closer and more snugly on top of my ears.

It took a little bit to get the hang of shaving. As I only have one eye, I have lost my depth perception. I also only see an area about the size of a dinner plate at any one time and do not have any peripheral fields of vision. Therefore, I do not try to hurry at all when shaving. I end up nicking myself enough as it is even if I go at a slow pace. Having this task done, I feel a lot better, but looking into the mirror, I still think I look like dung. However, it is the new me, and I am used to seeing dung-man in the mirror, so I move on to the shower.

As I am unable to stand without support, my shower is large enough to accommodate a bench that I sit on and shower with the use of a handheld showerhead. There are several grab rails inside the shower, so after I am done cleaning myself, the soap and shampoo part, I put the handheld showerhead into its slot and grab on tightly to the grab rails and let the water just wash over me for a couple of minutes while standing. It seems like such a small little thing, but it is really quite a big deal to me to be able to stand and have the water wash over me. I close my eyes and just enjoy the warmth for a minute or two. For a minute or two, I forget that I am handicapped at all. These are precious minutes for me.

Okay, time is up. The water goes off, and I grab a towel that I have already strategically put in a place where I will be able to grab it and dry off. I sit on the shower bench to do this. I then drop the towel on the floor of the shower to help me to keep from slipping and losing my balance as I get out of the shower. It does not take much for me to lose my balance. Therefore, I use every trick I can to improve my odds of not slipping and falling out of the shower.

Now dry, still naked, I do this next step every single morning at this very point. I weigh myself. I am six feet and one inch tall. I used to be a solid 185 pounds. Now, on a straight liquid diet of five cans of Ensure Plus each day, it is a battle to stay above 155 pounds. Every single pound is important to me, and it is essential that I know if I have lost a pound or two. Usually, I have a higher percentage of episodes where I black out and end up at urgent care getting stitches in my forehead or face if I drop below 155 pounds. So monitoring my weight is very crucial for me.

Next, to the medicine cabinet where I grab my pillbox, open the lid to the small box to the corresponding morning, and with the aid of a bottle of water I keep next to the sink, I swallow the fifteen pills I must take each morning to get me through the day.

Next, I clean my ear with a Q-tip and insert the hearing aid that I wear in my right ear. Now, for the first time since being awake, my world has sound to it. Prior to now, everything I have done has been done in total silence. It is nice to be able to hear now.

Now, some lotion and deodorant, and then I wash my hands. Next, I open the small container that is holding my prosthetic eye in some sterile solution, and without much effort at all, I place the eye in my eye socket and look into the mirror to ensure it is in straight.

Now, for the first time since waking, I look into the mirror and look like me, like a person and not a monster. Now, mentally, I think that I look and feel good.

It is a good feeling. Now onto getting dressed.

Getting dressed is very challenging for me. Depending on how I feel and what body parts are working dictates how long this will take, what I wear and, to some extent, if I will need help or not. I have been provided with aids to help me get dressed on my own by the veterans' hospital. I have a device that enables me to pull socks on my feet if my legs are not working well or if I cannot bend over. I have a multi-tool that I can grab and hold to help me snag zippers and pull them up. It also has a tool to grab buttons and pull them through button holes. Most of the time, this tool will just tear the buttons off my shirts. So I stay away from button-up shirts for the most part unless there is someone around to help me fasten the buttons. I then put on a watch, mostly for looks as I cannot see it well enough to read it; a ring or two; and a bracelet, which someone usually has to fasten for me. I slip on some boots and then back into the bathroom to comb my hair. I then attach the cochlear implant external device to the outside of my head where it says in place via a magnet embedded in my skull and an earpiece, or external processor rather, that sits on my ear.

I can now look in the mirror for a minute. The transformation from morning monster to the new me is now complete. I can hear. I feel pretty good. My day bathroom ritual is now complete.

To do all this takes me about an hour and a half.

I try to think of a positive thought for the day and then write it down on a notepad. Good morning to me! My day has now officially begun!

G.L. EWELL

Chapter Three

Homebound

Yeah, I have officially started my day! Now what? I feel all dressed up for the prom, but I am without a prom date. Now what, indeed? Oh, I know. I'll jump in the car and go to work.

Oh yeah, I forgot for a moment. I am permanently disabled. I am no longer employable and do not have a job. Well, remembering that little bit of reality sucks.

Oh, I know. I will jump in my truck and run down to the convenience store, say hello to some friends, and grab a cup of coffee—super idea!

Oh yeah, I forgot for a moment I can no longer drive. Because of my disabilities, the loss of feeling in my right leg, the tendency to fall asleep in a vehicle, and the fact that I am legally blind and have black-out episodes because of a few minor health problems, the state took away my driver's license. I will never get used to that. It just plain sucks! Especially when you live in a rural area where there is no public transportation.

I know there are those who are thinking right now, "Hey, if you hate it so bad out there in rural America without any public transportation, why don't you move to the city there, sport?" That is a possibility. It is one that I considered. I decided the pros to where I am living far outweighed the cons and therefore decided to stay. So I guess I will have to suck up that comment. I can do that. It does not take the sting out of the reality that I am also stuck at home. *Homebound* is what the Veterans Administration refer to this as. Unless I make arrangements to get a ride somewhere, right here at home is where I will stay.

So here I am all dressed up and nowhere to go. It doesn't take long for the thought to pop into my head, *Why did you even bother to get out of bed?* It is depressing as hell. It is also a thought I have struggled with for five years since my injuries. It has been five long years since I was blown up by roadside bombs in Iraq. I was an expert in the tactics and techniques the enemy was using to make to disguise and detonate their deadly improvised explosive devices (IEDs). It was my job to ensure the other teams who had the mission of looking for and rendering safe the deadly roadside bombs were all on the same sheet of music, so to speak. My job was to make sure they were all aware of the latest IED threats. This included ensuring they all knew the best tricks of the trade in employing the new equipment that we were being fielded to counterattack the improvised explosive devices. It was also my job to ensure information got to the proper training sites back stateside so that teams being trained to come to Iraq and perform this mission were receiving the very latest information from the battlefield so their skills would be honed against real threats, not outdated or techniques no longer used.

Yes, my vehicle was blown up six different times. Six different times by a bomb that was within three to ten feet from it. Six times by bombs so devastating the vehicle was destroyed, was no longer mission-capable.

Sometimes I think, as I am stuck at home without a ride, *Some damned expert I was.*

Yet I know I *was* one of the very best! At that particular time, the enemy was emplacing over 3,100 IEDs, or roadside bombs, every single month. Over one hundred every single stinking day! We (the combined efforts of the teams with this mission) were finding and rendering safe over 87 percent of them every month. We would tell one another that if we found a bomb, we just saved a life (usually, the reality was more than one). If we could find the enemy terrorists (I refuse to call the cowards, soldiers as they are not) who were emplacing the bombs and eliminate them, or have them surrender and taken as enemy combatant prisoners, we could save ten lives. If we could help provide the information to lead a team to a bomb maker, one hundred lives could be spared. Like with all criminals, they leave something telling about themselves at the crime scene, whether they know it or not. The same was true in Iraq. When we found a bomb, the area was treated a lot like a crime scene. That was after the fireworks were over and the area was safe enough to permit some kind of examination of the area around the bomb and the bomb itself, if it still existed, had been rendered safe.

But then, that was five years ago. Today, I am standing in my driveway with a cane in each hand to walk; looking at a vehicle I cannot drive or even see in its entirety with one glance because of my restricted sight.

I take in some of the morning for a minute longer and then go back inside.

Time to refill my morning coffee and think of a plan for the day. What will I do? I usually feel sorry for myself for a few more minutes before kicking myself mentally in the ass and telling myself I had better start counting blessings. For too many of my fallen brothers and sisters, just one bomb made them a memory. A name etched on a stone and placed somewhere that few will visit on a regular basis and many will forget as time passes, unfortunately. Every one of them is a hero. In my book, they are *all* heroes! None of them should be forgotten. But the sad truth is they will be.

When I was on active duty (army), I felt like I literally had five thousand close friends. After I became severely injured and was discharged, I found out I had close to five thousand acquaintances and about ten real friends, of which about five came by to see me. It was a very dark and depressing time during my recovery as the realization of that sat in, and I wondered what I would do with the rest of my life. What would I do indeed?

It was then that I realized that my war did not end when I became wounded. Neither did the personal wars of any severely wounded soldier. Our wars did not end on December 18, 2011, either, which is the date the war was officially declared over in Iraq. No, for the 32,226 of us that were wounded in that damned war, especially for the severely wounded, the day we were wounded was not the end of our war; it was just the beginning. The beginning to a war that has no end!

Every single day will be a new battle. Every single day will bring with it challenges to test our strength and resilience, both mentally and physically, as we learn to adapt to our new world with the physical and mental handicaps that now identify us. Every single day will bring the hurdle of depression to jump over and the hurdle of not feeling sorry for ourselves. Instead, look at what we can do and still have to be grateful for, look for ways we can still enjoy the lives we were spared and for ways to help one another to enjoy every day as well.

No matter how bad you have it, there is someone out there that has it worse off than you do and would give anything to be in your shoes.

Believe me, knowing that does not always make you feel like one lucky bastard. In fact, some days the depression hits so hard it is mighty tough to see anything beyond the scope of your own limitations. Especially as you remember the strong and healthy unchallenged person you used to be. Some days, the hurt and depression and the physical and mental pain is so overwhelming that suicide does not sound like all that bad of an option. I am being honest, and it is honestly a thought that has crossed my own mind more than once.

Thinking about suicide and acting upon it are two different things. I hate that so many of my brothers and sisters slipped to a place where they believed this was their only option and saw it through. It breaks my heart that so many were willing to put their very lives on the line to protect the freedoms so many take for granted only to find their cries for help went unnoticed.

Too many were allowed to slip through the cracks and fall mentally into a downward tailspin they could not pull out of. To realize only too late that they were hurting so badly and kept it so tightly bottled up that they could not be reached before they imploded in an act of senselessness that swept them away from us, is painful to me.

But that is a reality! A damned cold, hard reality of just how hard the war after the war really is!

It is also the only true end date to the war after the war for the severely injured—the day you die. Because every single day in between the day we became wounded and the day we die will be a challenge. Every single day will present to the severely wounded an obstacle to overcome, either mentally or physically—every single day!

Most will rise above the challenges, look for the beauty around them, count their blessings, and find ways to live happy and productive lives. Most will look for ways to help others despite the hardships they themselves face. And they will do it while simultaneously trying to find their own way down their own new path in life.

Many will discover how on their own as, for many, even their families move on. Divorce finds too many before they are able to find peace within themselves.

The recovery road is very difficult to navigate for a once strong and capable warrior who feared nothing in front of him while protecting all he loved behind him!

And this is the position I find myself now in while I think about how I will spend my day as I finish my coffee, realizing I do not have any appointments scheduled for today and likely will not have any visitors either.

Today will be just another day that I will try to find something productive to do so that I might be able to befriend someone besides depression and loneliness. One more swallow of coffee and realizing how many cups I have drunk, I realize it is time to go to the bathroom and use a catheter. Time once again to manually do that which I can no longer do: simply drain my bladder.

With the task at hand done—the draining of my bladder—it was time to get going about my day. I used to write a positive thought down on a piece of paper and carry it with me throughout the day. A simple positive thought about the value of friendship, a thought about love, perhaps a thought to help others who may be dealing with depression or PTSD, a thought about the healing power of God for those who believe in a higher power, or maybe even something humorous intended to bring a laugh or a smile. Anyway, I would write something down every morning. Even if it was simply one thing that I was thankful for on any particular day that I could say out loud or think about if dark thoughts came into my head or cold feelings into my heart. Some little thought I could pull out of my pocket and read if I started to feel my demons from war sneak up on me or if my old friend depression tries to get me to open up the door and let him in. This little practice has evolved over the years.

Instead of writing a thought on some random piece of paper, napkin, paper towel, or candy wrapper of some kind, I post my positive thought on the Internet on my Facebook page almost daily.

It has turned into quite a little project and something that quite a few people look forward to every day. A few even let me know when I skip a day.

So I will spend an hour or two on the computer. First, I will post my positive thought for the day on the internet. I usually get quite a bit of feedback right away. I will know almost instantly if my thought was one that inspired others or if I tanked it; meaning, I bombed for the day with my post on my Facebook page.

I have learned to use Facebook as a barometer for my daily postings. If more than fifty people across the country click that they like my daily post and a lot comment on it or share it on their own page, I will put it aside in a file on the computer for use somewhere down the road. I may use it in a book I am writing, or perhaps I will incorporate it into a public speech I am scheduled to give at one place or another. I will consider it a tested and proven comment on whatever subject I have based the comment upon, like friendship or love, just as a couple of examples. I will know immediately if it my post was not a very popular one or well received and immediately send it to the boneyard—the Recycle Bin on the computer, that is

I began calling my little posts Gordy-isms. My nickname is Gordy, and the term *Gordy-isms* just kind of stuck. I include some of them in the books I write.

One day I will publish a book of nothing but Gordy-isms, one for every day of the year perhaps.

Believe me when I tell you that I do not think it would ever make a best seller list anywhere. However, it is kind of fun, requires some positive thinking, and is a good way to get some creative energy flowing.

I then will check my e-mail and return e-mails to any that require a follow-up or a reply back to or any that I feel merit a personal response. I still stay in contact with a lot of soldiers who are doing route clearance missions in Afghanistan and will often be asked my opinion about something or a certain scenario that could possibly happen or be encountered on the battlefield.

It is funny. I have no memory of any Christmases that have ever passed, not a single one. Even looking at photos brings up a big blank, nothing for me. I used to be good at math, college math, as I was seeking a science degree. Now, I cannot do the simple math required to manage a checkbook or even know how to count change back to someone. I know what a quarter, nickel, dime, and penny is. However, none of the coins mean anything of value to me. I could not add them or even tell you how many you would need for a soda machine.

Yet combat tactics and techniques are burned into my brain or located in just the right place in my mind that they remain sharp as a tack. I have not only retained the knowledge but built upon it based upon things I read and hear from soldiers on the ground in Afghanistan.

Anyway, I will spend some time on the computer. The Veterans Administration has provided me with a computer specially built for my restricted and poor vision. It has a giant screen and a program that will make everything very large for me to see. It will also speak to me if I need help or get stuck somewhere and do not remember how to do something. It is a huge help for me. It also helps keep me in touch with the world inaccessible to me when I am unable to leave my house or yard without assistance. It helps to make being homebound more bearable on some days that are harder than others.

Next I move on to some simple home-maintenance tasks or light cleaning chores that I am able to do. You learn to be a pretty good shopper at the store or at least have on hand a little something of everything you can think of. For instance, if you were in the middle of a project and run out of something, you are just flat screwed if you don't have extra on hand. When you are home bound, if you don't have it, tough luck. Because you certainly cannot just jump in your vehicle and run to the store and grab whatever you need when you need it. If you don't have it, you go without it until your next store day unless you get lucky and find someone who can take you to get what you need or bring you what you need. Whatever you are doing comes to a complete stop, and you move on if you run out of something. Being homebound, you learn you must keep plenty on hand. You must make sure you have what you need to get by in case of an emergency—a power outage, a natural disaster, or whatever you can think of because when it happens, you are on your own.

Without power, you cannot even call someone for help. So you had better make sure you have a plan in place or someone to check in on you regularly. If not and you have an accident, hurt, or just plain in need of something, you could be without help or something you may be in need of for a very long time. It is a lesson you do not want to have to learn via the School of Hard Knocks.

It is somewhat of a blow to your pride to be so reliant on others, especially after being a warrior trained to get by with what you have available to you; to adapt and overcome; and to improvise, be creative, and do whatever it takes to get the job done, to get the mission accomplished. The mission is everything. To not succeed is nothing short of failure. Failure on the battlefield means someone just got killed or someone was left in a dire situation without help, reinforcements, or much-needed supplies. An area that needs to be cleared of hazards or a passage not cleared just put others in danger. No, nothing short of mission accomplishment is acceptable. After twenty-four years of military service, that carries over into your life after the service. Everything has its place, and when you find you do not have everything you need, you adapt and overcome—a very useful mind-set when handicapped and homebound. No matter what, you adapt and overcome, even if your mission is simply a house-cleaning task or doing a simple load of laundry.

Your mission could be just getting through the day by winning the war against depression; getting through the day without fighting demons that followed you home from war uninvited and refuse to leave is a big deal.

It may not feel like it, but just accomplishing that on some days is a very big deal.

One thing to remember is that you will not win every battle. You will not succeed in every mission you set out to do. Especially in the beginning as you learn to deal with your handicaps. This was perhaps the hardest thing for me to put into perspective. It was one of the hardest things for me to understand and learn. There are some things that I just am not physically or mentally able to do anymore. That I can no longer do them does not mean I have failed. It does not mean I did not accomplish my mission. It simply means that I am not physically or mentally capable of doing some things now that I used to be able to do. And that is okay. It is not my fault. I was blown up, for god's sake. There was nothing I could have done different. It was not my fault. It just happened. It happened at war. And I survived!

Now it is essential that I realize, and others like me realize, there are some things we just can no longer do. And that's okay. It is also okay to ask for help when you need it. It is not a sign of weakness or failure to complete a mission by asking for help. In fact, it is a sign of good judgment that you have learned to realize your limitations and boundaries and learned to use them to your advantage. And it does not put yourself in danger by trying to do things beyond them.

Accepting your limitations and handicaps in no way means that you give up, that you quit trying to move forward, or that you do not try to push yourself to achieve new heights. It is not a compromise either.

It is simply acknowledging that you do not have the ability or capabilities you had before you were injured. It does not mean that you lack the strength, courage, or the commitment to push yourself to new heights and levels of excellence. It simply means you must learn to use everything you still have available to you to be the best you can be.

I may not be able to jog every morning ever again, but I might become a damned good swimmer instead.

Being homebound, I may not be able to drive to work ever again. But I am capable of doing things at home to occupy my time and my mind. I can think and write. I can try writing books in an attempt to help others who are suffering through some of the things I have. I can learn to draw or paint and create something to hang on someone's wall that would bring happiness to him or her. I can take care of a small garden or do volunteer work to help others. I can chase a college degree by taking online courses right at home. Being homebound does not have to be a life sentence or a negative thing. It just means you have to change your outlook on how you view things, change the angle of your perspective a bit. And therein lays the challenge. Once you have gotten that figured out in a positive light, you accomplish your mission. You will have met your objective and have become victorious again!

I have engaged the enemy in each city listed on these signs. More than once I found a bomb under the bridge in the distance. The sign on the left reads Fallujah; the one on the right reads Baghdad. When I was there, both roads led to the same place: hell!

Chapter Four

Going Somewhere

Once a soldier is severely wounded in combat, from that very second forward, the war after the war begins. This war after the war will not have an end date. I take that back; it will have an end date. The date will be etched in granite or some other stone or upon a plate of bronze that is affixed in one way or another to the soldier's final resting spot. I guess many people's remains are put to rest, if you will, in different ways according to their religious beliefs or their own personal last wishes; I guess it would be more accurate to say that you will be able to find the date of their war after the war ends on their death certificate. It is just a reality.

So many are so severely wounded they will battle the rest of their lives to fit in to the world they now belong to and will belong to for the rest of their lives. The paralyzed soldier is not going to wake up one day and find that he can use his limbs again. The severely brain-damaged soldier is not going to wake up twenty years from now and suddenly have a perfectly functioning brain. Every day will present challenges. Every day, there will be a battle to be won or lost! They may be big battles in the beginning and likely become smaller and smaller battles as time goes on, but every day, there will be a battle, large or small, to adapt to and overcome. Each day, mentally or physically, a battle will be fought.

There are two weapons that will be force equalizers, which will help determine the outcome of each battle. They are attitude and heart. Loved ones and family will be a big factor, obviously. However, when it gets right down to it, only you, the wounded soldier, will be at the tip of the spear in your own personal battles. You—and only you—will see the demons that might try to find you at night or when you are alone. Family and loved ones will be able to lay a solid foundation for you if they have the will, love, and desire—which, sadly, many don't. If you have that solid foundation to build upon, you are blessed. Your chances of winning battles will increase dramatically. However, with or without that solid foundation, when it comes right down to it, you—and only you—will find out if you have the attitude and heart required to fight every fight and stay engaged long enough to win those battles. You ultimately will be the one that decides how hard and long you fight your own war after the war.

The second you became a casualty, it started. Then and there, the path you were traveling in life got slammed closed with a big old barricade and a huge detour sign that directs you to a new road to travel—a crappy unimproved, unmaintained, often uncharted road full of obstacles, bumps, cracks, potholes, and ruts—lots of ruts. The road is called the recovery road. The road sucks! It varies in length for everyone. But it starts the same for everyone as well. It sucks! I can think of a whole page of swear words I would love to type to describe how horrid, painful, scary, and miserable it is. Mentally and physically, pain, sorrow, depression, and fatigue will fill most of your time as you begin to travel down recovery road.

Everyone's recovery road has distinct stages to it. For instance, there is the initial aid you are provided by a Combat Lifesaver, medic, or navy corpsman immediately. Seconds may seem like hours, hours spent in hell. You are then transported, one way or another—ground or air—to a medical facility. More time in hell as you are operated on or otherwise stabilized enough to be able to the make the flight out of country. You may have spent time in Germany. Eventually, you end up stateside in a military or VA hospital. Perhaps at one and then transported on to the other. In any case, each one of these stops, each move forward from one place to another, is a definitive stage—or mile marker, if you will—down your recovery road. Eventually, you end up at a facility where you will spend most of your initial recovery.

It is here, at this stage, when the magnitude of what has happened to you sets in. It is here when you realize or you are told or you come to understand that your life will never be the same. You know the extent of your injuries, and you know how permanent the damage is. You may not accept it as fact yet, but you know.

To get to this point, you will have survived. You have fought hard with everything within you, with your heart and your desire to live. You have gotten through the initial hell that can be found at every turn at the beginning of the road. You have proven that you have the attitude and heart needed to navigate the road. Now what?

You move on to the next stage: recovery and rehabilitation. You may have more operations.

You might have to suffer through the hell of being treated for burns. Or you might have to endure the confusion from serious brain injuries.

Here is when the reality sets in. Now is when it hits you right smack in the face that you will never be the same person again. Now is when the reality really sets in and shoves out the door the denial you may have been in about the extent of your injuries.

By now, you are where those you love, or some of them anyway, are able to be with you. It is now that you see it in their faces, though they try to hide it, that they know you will never be the same again—ever! At this point, along with the trauma and everything else you are going through, suddenly, a big dump truck full of depression gets heaped upon you. You are at a stage now where worry and doubt decide to join depression and gang-rape you. As if dealing with your traumatic injuries were not enough, now you get to dwell in every moment that you are alone with your thoughts, not only about how your injuries will affect you for the rest of your life but also about how your injuries are going to affect those you care about and love for the rest of your life.

Believe me. I know that, at this stage, it is not positive images that get painted on the walls inside your brain. You begin to wonder if a wife, husband, boyfriend, or girlfriend will still love you. You wonder if people dear to you in your life will choose to stay in your life. Far too often, there are those who find out that someone they love and care about will make a decision that the road is not one they have the strength to go down with you.

Soldiers find that some people are not up to the task, and they move on. Divorce is astronomically high for the severely disabled soldier. It does not matter why or who is to blame for it happening. The sad fact is that it does happen. If it does happen to you, then the stage is set for more depression, anger, and fear to accompany you down your recovery road.

Attitude and heart—here you will find just how much both of you have to continue to press forward.

Even if loved ones do not leave you, you begin to wonder and question if they will. You wonder if someone could really love you, be honest and faithful to you in your busted, broken, or burned up condition.

More doubt to haunt your thoughts. More doubt to set in and create a fertile field to plant and grow seeds of depression, fear, and mistrust.

Now you must decide where you are going, in addition to trying to focus on getting better and getting back everything you possibly can during your recovery and endless therapies.

It is here where battles will be fought hardest as you have to find the inner strength to believe relationships will remain intact. This is when you have to have faith that they will. Here is when you will know and find out if love is unconditional or based upon a weaker foundation of merely a physical attraction. If physical elements of a relationship are stronger than the substance of true love, you may find yourself alone.

Then what? Will you have the attitude and heart to keep fighting battles? Where will you go then? Will you have the strength mentally to stay in the fight?

Will you have the heart to keep pressing forward in your recovery? Only you can decide if you press forward.

So what are you going to do? Attitude and heart—do you have enough of both? Are you strong enough to adapt and overcome? Do you have the vision to see into the future in such a way that you know you will be okay? Do you have the faith to see that, down the road, things will get better for you? If you don't, it is just a matter of time before the grim reaper will come knocking on your door.

So are you going somewhere? Are you going to be able to keep fighting the good fight?

If you do, you'll find out that everything has a way of working out. It may not be at the light speed you would like it to, but a day at a time, one battle at a time. If you can somehow find something to keep you positive and focused, you will be fine. You will never be the same old you. You can forget that person. You will never be that person again—not ever!

So are you going somewhere? Are you going to get stuck in a rut of depression?

Only you can find the inner strength to keep moving forward. Only you can get it in your mind that you can keep moving. You can press forward and find your new self. You can be productive doing something again.

You can find many good reasons to keep pushing forward if you want to. There is a whole world of beauty that is waiting for you. There is a whole world of people who need you, who will need to rely upon you getting through this, getting out of the depression rut, over the hump and moving forward again in the positive light of self-worth.

So are you giving up, or are you going somewhere?

Adapt and overcome. You have places to go!

Chapter Five

Get a Life

It has been five years since I was literally blown up in Iraq. The first three years of my recovery road were brutal. It was a very intense time as I bounced from three different states, being admitted for extensive hospital stays in three different hospitals. There was a six-month stay in an assisted-living facility and shorter hospital stays in seven different hospitals for nine follow-up surgeries. I was treated by forty-seven different health care specialists during this time. It was hell, both physically and mentally. When I was not admitted into a hospital, I was being driven every day for medical appointments and therapies at our veterans' hospital. There were medical treatment facilities in the private sector that were treating me as well. All of which were a one-hour drive, one way, to get to. It was a very hard, physically and mentally demanding time as they were putting Humpty Dumpty back together again.

During this time, my life was literally nothing but a medical something or other. Going to medical appointments and therapies was my life. It was my job, so to speak. It was what I did at least five times a week.

Now I have reached a plateau in my medical treatments. This basically means I have got to a point where this is me. The rebuilding is over. Now, it is more a matter of maintaining the work. There is little more they can do for me that would give me back any more of the physical capabilities that I lost.

My brain damage has got to a point where testing, testing, and more testing has shown that my brain is not going to ever magically surprise everyone and get any better. The damage I have now is considered permanent, and the residual effects of my traumatic brain injury are going to be handicaps I will live with for the rest of my life.

As I mentioned, my medical treatment plan has now shifted from recovery and rehabilitation to maintenance. I still have some major dental and oral surgery work to be done, as well as continuing to have speech therapy twice a week and mental health therapy scheduled at least once a week. A chemical balance has finally been reached, as far as the medicines I need to be on, to prevent seizures, tremors, and uncontrollable motor movements. The right doses of narcotics have been discovered for a long-term chronic-pain plan that will keep me from being in so much pain I cannot function, yet left with pain that I can live with and tolerate without taking so much that I will be loopy, stoned, or in a state that I cannot exercise good judgment and reason.

I will never be pain-free. However, I will be able to have my pain controlled enough that I can get out and about and still be able to enjoy life. I will be able to interact in my new world, even with its definitive limitations and boundaries.

My post-traumatic stress syndrome is still at a severity level that is disrupting my life. Too often my demons from war will prevent me from sleeping at night.

Rarely do I get the rest my body so desperately needs. Most of my sleep comes in the form of little catnaps during the day.

I will always be dependent on my blind man's cane when walking. I will always require the use of a support cane or wheelchair to get around. I will never be able to drive again and, thus, will always be dependent on others to get out of the house and get to appointments, to the store, to do my business errands, or to meetings, and to get out of the house just simply for recreation.

I will always have limited vision and be classified as legally blind. I will always be deaf without the use of my cochlear implant and a hearing aid.

I will always require the use of a catheter to drain my bladder. There will not be a day that goes by that I will be completely free of medications, which I will need mentally to maintain a normal way of life as normal will ever be for me.

I will always have problems with my gait (walking). As I am always at risk of blacking out or falling, I will need to wear a damned helmet when out and about to prevent further injury to my brain when these episodes happen.

The bottom line is, I am permanently disabled. I will never be able to have a full-time job again. My life now will always have set boundaries and limitations.

I may never be able to have a regular job again, but that does not mean I cannot have a life. And that is where I am at now—trying to figure out my life.

A job helps a person feel productive. Just because I will never be able to have a regular job in the workforce of America does not mean that I cannot be productive.

Being productive and feeling like you have things you have to do each and every day is essential to fighting off major disabling depression, depression that is so destructive it can turn into drug and alcohol abuse and further lead one into a downward spiral that could also lead to self-destruction or suicide. A downward spiral that usually also leads to the destruction of family and marital relationships. It further leads to the loss of friendships, and if the downward spiral does not stop, an eventual life of loneliness and despair is what will await you.

So get a life!

Yes, easy to say, but hard as hell to figure out what to do the rest of your life when you are severely disabled.

So what to do with the rest of my life? A good question that I wish I had a definite answer for. If I had that answer, the quality of my life would improve. It is a simple fact.

Up to now, the first stage of my life after being severely wounded in combat consisted of one thing and one thing only: trying to get better. My job every day was to try to get back as much of the old me as possible. My job, if you will, was basically survival.

Trying to recover and rebound from one surgery to get to the next and trying to get through one rehabilitation therapy and on to the next was my job.

As I continued to gain more abilities, mentally and physically, more opportunities would present themselves.

In the beginning, I literally had medical appointments all day long. As time went by and my abilities improved, there began to be gaps in my appointments. I would be at the VA hospital, and after finishing up with an appointment, I would find that I had one or two hours before the next therapy. I would fill this time by visiting the wounded and sick who were bedridden. This eventually led me to the volunteer service manager at the VA hospital. She came up with the idea of having me push a cart around to veterans who were bedridden at the hospital. On my cart, I would have small craft kits, magazines, and crossword-puzzle books. I would also take any requests for items the bedridden veterans had, go get them, and bring them back to them. Volunteering began to fill some of that void—or need, rather—to feel productive. It also led to more volunteer work.

Before long, I not only joined but became a lifetime member of every military service organization I could afford to. I attended every single meeting and function that I possibly could. I was even elected to be the senior vice commander of my Disabled American Veterans (DAV) chapter (Wasatch One, in Utah) and the vice president of the Blue Star Riders (based out of Oakley, California).

The more I did, the more I wanted to do. It was giving my life purpose. Volunteering and helping others was therapeutic in that I began to feel productive. It was becoming my job. It was replacing the old job of just fighting to get through each day. As time went by, I found myself wanting to do even more.

I was soon committing to doing speaking engagements.

I told myself I would never turn down an opportunity to talk about patriotism, respect for our flag, soldiers, or wounded warriors and veterans. I was soon speaking at local public and private schools, to Scout troops at public events, and to Rotary clubs and Chambers of Commerce. However, it soon began to seem as if the speaking engagements came in streaks. It was not very regular, and soon I was wondering what else I could do.

I had been writing quite a bit as part of my PTSD therapy under the direction of my PTSD counselor. I was getting quite a collection of poems I had written about my own PTSD as well as my combat tour of duty in Iraq. Often, I would share some of my writing with other veterans. I was getting positive feedback, which made me want to keep writing. It also was helping me fight some of my own demons as I continued to battle with my PTSD.

The suicide rate among soldiers during this time was staggering. Eighteen soldiers a day were committing suicide. That so many of my brothers and sisters were falling through the cracks and getting to a place of despair where suicide became the only option for them was disturbing to me. I felt as if I had to do something.

But what could I do? Many times during recovery, hell, the thought crossed my mind. But never did I get to a point that I would have carried through with it. Yet I did know what it felt like to hurt so badly, both physically and mentally, that the thought had crossed my mind. I now knew what more I could do. If I could somehow put some of those thoughts and feelings into words, maybe—just maybe—someone who was hurting like that could read them and know they were not alone. Maybe just the knowledge that someone else felt like they did and could get through it would help them. If I could do this and keep just one of my brothers or sisters from committing suicide, it would be worth it. I knew it was something I had to try to do. I had to try to help. I had found another job. I knew I had traveled down a road that gave me the ability to reach out to others traveling down similar roads of hell and could use what little encouragement or advice I could offer to them from having traveled down such roads.

It was not an easy task. Just reliving memories and feelings that I was trying to bury was brutal. But how could I honestly reach out to someone without being brutally honest in writing about the feelings I had felt and experienced when I had those same thoughts of despair enter my mind? I had to recall those horrid thoughts in order to accurately account for them and write them down. It was not an easy thing to do at all.

It took the better part of a year to write. There were many times I did not think it would get done. But with encouragement from others and hard work, it got done.

With the financial help of some angels, it got published. It is entitled *Dung in My Foxhole*.

So maybe I will be a writer. Here I am writing my second book and have started a third as well.

What else can I do? I have always enjoyed doodling a bit; maybe I will try painting. I will learn how to prepare a canvas and try to do some oil painting. Perhaps I will do some pencil sketches as well.

It can also help if you have a hobby or if you can find something you are interested in collecting and start a collection of something. I have started to collect old coins and books.

It does not matter what you collect or if you paint or draw. Perhaps you might put model cars or planes together or start doing photography. You might even try raising a small garden of flowers or vegetables if you are able and have some space to do it.

The bottom line is that you have got to do something! If you don't, you will find depression knocking on your door in a hurry. Depression leads straight to despair. Despair, without getting any help, leads straight to one place and one place only. Don't even think about it.

Get a life! Get productive! Find whatever it is that you can enjoy and can give you purpose and a feeling of productivity. Find whatever it is that you can think of or refer to as your job.

Remember, at first, it might be that your job is simply getting from one surgery to the next. It might be just getting through one therapy and on to the next. But you will get beyond that stage. Adapt and overcome!

What if you are paralyzed? What if you are paralyzed from the neck down? So what! Get a life!

Easy for me to say when I have working limbs, right?

Wrong! It is not easy to say. It is not easy for you to do if you are paralyzed. Hell, it is not even easy to hear if you are paralyzed. But you have to do it. And there are still ways you can fill your days with joy and feel productive. I don't claim to have all the answers. I don't claim to even know all the questions, but I do know this: you have to find something that will enable you to find some peace and happiness. You have to find something that will enable you to feel productive.

There is someone out there who needs your help. Someone needs you to mentor them. Somebody is waiting to hear what you have to say that will help them to navigate in their recovery road. They will get to a place down their road near hell and find bumps and ruts that only you will be able to help them get through. Don't let them down. We leave no one behind, remember? You can do it. Adapt and overcome!

There are two things I want you to remember. First, no matter how bad you think you have it, I promise you, someone has it worse. Second, there is a higher power that can help you. Have faith and call upon it. I call it God. So what are you waiting for now? Get a life!

G.L. EWELL

Essayons!
(Meaning, "Let us try!")

Iron Cross

Chapter Six

It Takes a Team

There is so much going on at once for the severely wounded soldier that it is difficult to isolate and diagnose some problems because many share overlapping symptoms. This is especially true when you get into dealing with your mental well-being or trying to isolate specific mental health problems or disorders.

I am *not* a trained or board certified mental health professional or social worker in any way, shape, or form. I do not claim to be nor have a desire to be one.

What I do claim is to be a severely wounded combat veteran with multiple severe physical and mental health traumatic injuries that had to be dealt with immediately, some that took several years to get on top of and many issues that are ongoing, which I continue to deal with.

What I offer here is food for thought that has come from my own victories and failures, ups and downs, as well as highs and lows of some aspects of dealing with my own injuries after being injured in combat in the war in Iraq.

I have learned it takes a team, in my opinion, to be successful in overcoming multiple traumatic injuries. You have physical traumatic injuries as well as mental traumatic injuries that must be dealt with. Therefore you will be dealing with medical doctors and mental health professionals. They are both part of *your* team. Hey, but what about you? Only *you* know what *you* are feeling or not feeling. So *you* are part of the team. Do not forget that. Be vocal. Let everyone know what you feel, how it feels, and when you feel it.

For the medical and mental health professionals to be as effective as they possibly can, they are going to need *your* feedback. The quicker they get it, the faster they can make necessary adjustments or changes to strategies they may employ to get you back to the best you they possibly can.

There is also another part of the team. Who that team member is depends on your individual living circumstances. If you are married, the other team member will be your spouse. If you are single, it might be a parent, roommate, significant other (a boyfriend or girlfriend), or a caregiver. There is someone around you during your recovery. The simple fact is that there are times you will not always be cognizant of your actions. You may not know what you are doing as you sleep, for instance. You may have episodes where you stop breathing momentarily. You may kick and thrash about in bed all night. There may be sleepwalking or nightmares you act out or talking or screaming in your sleep. These are just a few examples of things that you could not tell someone as you would not know yourself of such activities. But believe me, someone you are living with and sharing life with will know about every single one. It is important that they share this knowledge and information. It is vital input. This is why it is important that you acknowledge them as a vital part of your recovery team too. It is also imperative that you have trust in them. They may relate things that you may not believe you do. They may say things you may not like to hear. But you have to let them be said and heard. If you can't trust them to tell the truth about things, you have no way of knowing differently; the reality is, maybe you need to rethink your living arrangements. Time is a key factor in all the many phases of your recovery. You need to work as a team. You need to have faith in *your team*! That means you must *trust* in what is being said by people who love and care about you, who want to see you regain as much good health as you possibly can. No one wants to see you suffer. Have faith in *your team*. Work together as a *team*. Be as proactive as you possibly can be in letting all the professionals who are part of your get-well team know about everything going on with you. Don't just assume that your primary care doctor knows what your orthopedic doctor is doing. Let them both know what the other is having you do or not do. Don't assume an optometrist knows what your audiologist is doing for you. They don't. Help them out. The worst thing that can happen is everyone stays informed. What is wrong with that? What you don't want is vital information slipping through the cracks, which could affect the effectiveness of specialized treatments you may be receiving. Communicate openly about how you are feeling—your pain, your appetite, whatever! Do not assume that something is not important to the doctors. If you have a question, ask it. If you feel funny or unsure about something, anything, say so. Everything must be considered as relevant and vital information that could prove to be very instrumental to professionals on your team. Remember, it is your health. If you are unable to communicate or relate information, it is imperative that whoever is aiding you is vocal about passing information on about things like your sleeping habits, eating habits, how much or how little sleep you are getting, and your overall mood or demeanor. You never know what little bit of information is just what a doctor is looking for to make an adjustment to or change a medication. If you can't communicate details like these, someone needs to. Somebody needs to be able to watch, observe, and witness your actions, reactions, habits, and moods in order to assist your get-well team in being as effective as possible for you. The number of times you go to the bathroom is important as well as the color of your urine and the consistency of your stools when you poop. Laugh if you want to, but it is all extremely important information to a specialist, especially if they are trying to determine how efficiently your digestive system is working. Especially if they are worried about how well your kidneys or liver are functioning. Now is not the time to be shy or silly about saying out loud in front of anyone, especially your doctors, if it is hard to poop or if it burns when you urinate. Penis, balls, gonads, dick, anus, ass, rectum, vagina, clitoris, pussy, crotch, groin—*whatever*! It is going to hurt, burn, itch, get a rash, or be sensitive. When it does, say it. Don't be shy! It could be a sign of an adverse reaction to a medicine. Who knows? But if you don't say something because you are too immature to describe your body and what is going on with it to someone, you are taking serious risks that could be putting yourself in danger!

Information is knowledge. The more feedback and information everyone on the team has, the more knowledgeable the decisions will be that will affect your speedy recovery, or lack thereof.

It is not just the doctors that need information either. Remember, it is a recovery team. It is *your team*.

If you do not understand something, ask a question. Don't be afraid to tell someone to talk slower or look at you when they are talking. You need to understand clearly the instructions you are given. You need to understand clearly why you are doing or not doing something or why you are taking or not taking a medication. You need information as well. So does your spouse or whoever is helping you during your recovery. If they don't understand something, let them ask a question. Even if you know the answer, let them ask their own questions so they are clear. Remember, they may need to react in the event you are not coherent. You could have a seizure. You could have a fall and be unconscious. You could have an adverse reaction to a medicine or have an accidental overdose or have medicines that do not react well together. That other team member, the person sharing your life or looking after you, needs all the knowledge they can get too. And after all, what is the worst thing that could happen? That everyone knows what the goals and expected outcome of your treatment is; sounds like a good deal to me.

Everything I listed above has happened to me. That is why I know everyone needs to understand one another.

I was a bomb hunter in Iraq. A vehicle I was in was blown up on six different occasions. I suffered a severe traumatic brain injury. I broke my neck and damaged my vertebrae in my lower spine. I lost my hearing, an eye, and my balance system. I had, and still have, neurological problems. I would shake uncontrollably in the early stages of my recovery. I had seizures. I have blacked out and fallen and split my head open fifty-nine separate times, which required me to go to urgent care or the hospital emergency room, and required ten or more stitches each of those fifty-nine times to close the head wound. I have had extreme weight loss that made medications react differently. I have visited places of extremely high elevations that made my medications react differently. I have forgotten I took my medicines and taken them again and ended up in the intensive care unit (ICU) of the hospital for five days. I stop breathing at night and now require a CPAP machine with oxygen at night. I had restless leg syndrome. I would walk in my sleep at night. Hell, I would even leave the house and be wandering aimlessly outside in my sleep. I have been found under the kitchen table asleep, in closets, and even under the house. I would be asleep and wandering about, acting out missions I did in combat. It is a good thing someone was able to not only witness my actions but also know what to do when I would display them; otherwise, they would have occurred. Otherwise, I might not be here. I could not have told a doctor that my breathing stopped, and I had to be physically shaken to get me to gasp for a breath of air. You need someone to relay information to the professionals on your team for them to be able to counteract them. Your caregiver needs to know how to react in the event something like that happens.

That is why I believe so strongly that it takes team effort, and everyone on the team needs to clearly understand and be able to relate information back and forth to one another.

The more complex that your injuries are, the more people there will be on your recovery team.

Establishing good communication skills between everyone on your recovery team right from the start will greatly enhance the quality of your care and eliminate some trial and error in some instances.

It is a plain truth, a simple fact. Make it happen!

G. L. EWELL

A Dead Man's Hand
Don't let depression ruin your life.

Chapter Seven

Depression Will Find You

It is not a matter of *if* or *when* but rather how hard it will hit and how long it will last. Depression is an ugly monster that, unfortunately, comes with the trauma of being severely wounded, or wounded at all for that matter. It hides at every casualty evacuation point, every medical treatment facility, and in every patient-care facility. There is not a hospital wing, ward, or room where it does not lurk in. It roams freely from intensive care units to patient-recovery rooms. It follows the wounded soldier and those who eventually come to be at their side through every stage of recovery. There is not a safe place to hide from it. There is no place it is not allowed to rear its ugly head. It does not discriminate. It will climb on board with you during your recovery just as soon as it can and will stay for as long as possible. It will make your recovery harder, and it is very contagious. Once it has climbed on board with you or with those who are around you every day, it is easily transferred from one to another and, in fact, gets passed back and forth between people many times if it is allowed to. Depression is a monster that is hard to kill. If allowed, it will just keep resurfacing, and it usually does, time after time after time.

No one is immune.

Everyone will feel the effects of the beast that depression is and has to figure out how to fight it.

The wounded warriors, already weakened by the trauma of both physical and mental wounds and scars of war, and everyone that loves and cares about them will have to battle depression at one point or another. The fight with depression will be difficult at best. It strikes hard, without warning, and will not be easy to break free from.

Depression will complicate the wounds one has to recover from and make the recovery process even more difficult than it already is.

It will not only make recovering from your wounds harder, it will inflict more of them to recover from. Depression will inflict a whole new set of injuries that will need to be dealt with. It will intensify the recovery from your physical wounds and complicate the recovery of the mental injuries, which you have to deal with as well. To make things even worse, it will probably add more mental and emotional wounds and trauma, which will need to be diagnosed, recognized, acknowledged, and tended to in order to swiftly counterattack and prevent its spreading throughout each stage of your recovery. It will need to be treated immediately so that your focus can return to the healing of the initial wounds that were inflicted by the hands of the enemy or the enemy's instruments of war.

Depression will cloud you from being able to see a future beyond that of the initial pain you are struggling to overcome. It will create a diversion, which will prevent you from seeing a future with a happy ending to it that is essential to your recovery and moving forward through each stage of it successfully.

Believe me; I am not trying to depress anyone by telling you these things. I do so only as a warning so that everyone might be prepared and ready to strike back hard at the depression monster with a good, strong knockout punch when he decides to make an appearance. Don't fool yourself. You are not immune. He will make an appearance. Remember, it is not *if*, it is *when*.

I have personally had several fights with the depression monster. I know too well of the strangle hold he can get on a person. His grip is strong and can suffocate the will to live right out of you if you are not prepared. More than once, he has tried to push thoughts of suicide into my head. I thank God that suicide only got as far as just a thought in my head. I am also angry that I let him get so far as to get that thought into my head. But he is very skilled in his dark profession. He also has many friends that help him sneak up on you and ambush you when you will be at a point along your recovery road that is advantageous for him.

It is very important that you know a few of his friends. Know them well so that you can stay away from them. He will usually send them in first to wear you down and weaken you so that his job will be easy. However, if you can avoid their snares, pitfalls, and poisonous bites, your chances of avoiding him or defeating him when he does show his ugly head are increased dramatically.

Depression is very good friends with loneliness, despair, and self-pity. He hangs out with shattered dreams, doubt, and hopelessness.

Together they steal and try to take away all your faith, love, and trust—both in others as well as yourself.

They are infamous for repeatedly posting questions in your mind like "Why me? Why keep fighting? What is there to live for? Who could love me like this?"

Trying to repeatedly throw up images of the horror, ugliness, brutality, and inhumanity of war that you have witnessed, experienced, tasted, and lived through is something they all thrive on, laugh at, and get a thrill out of as they watch you fall deeper into a bottomless pit of mental anguish and darkness from which they will make you believe that there can be no relief or way to get out.

Filling your mind with the smoke of confusion, to blind you from seeing the light of love and the outstretched hands of so many who are desperately trying to help you, is just one of many things they have mastered.

Your tears will seem endless. It will be a choking chore to try to get enough air into your lungs to breathe. Your heart will feel as though it is going to explode within the very walls of your chest. Hot flashes and sweat and fever will instantly change to the chills and shakes from what feels like a bitter ice storm in your very soul.

Your silent screams for help, mercy, and relief from all the mental torment will seem to fall upon deaf ears and be unheard.

All this endless bombardment of mental torture and the hellish sounds of the iron-clad chains to which you feel shackled, all this and more than you can imagine will beat down upon you as wave after never-ending wave from the sea of devastation and destruction restlessly pounds against you. All this and more will occur simultaneously while you are trying to battle with the extreme physical pain from your wounds.

Does it sound impossible for anyone to handle alone?

Your odds of getting hit by lightning are better than your odds of successfully doing it alone is what I would tell you!

However you look at it, at best, it is going to be a walk through hell, again, as you make your journey through the many different stages of your own never-ending recovery road.

Depression is a horrible monster that cannot be ignored. It is imperative that you and everyone around you realize this. There is never going to be a place or a time that you will be immune to depression.

Depression will never be but a step or two behind you, just waiting for you to stumble, get weak or weary as you make your way down this new path of life that is yours to travel. Like it or not, the path was selected for you the moment you became a casualty of war.

Like it or not, it is a reality that you must come to terms with.

As a wounded warrior, you need to accept that this will be a lifetime battle. You need to *know* that it is a battle that not only you will fight, but those that love and care about you will have to fight it as well. Depression is now a monster that will chase after your loved ones and those you care about for the rest their lives as well or for as long as they are connected to you. The time will come that you will need to be strong for them.

For those who love and care about their wounded warrior, you will need to be strong and be on the lookout for depression in them. Know also and understand that the depression monster has you on his list to attack as well. You need to be prepared to fight off depression not only for them but for yourself as well.

Everyone in America needs to realize that for our country's wounded warriors, their family, friends, and everyone in their support network, depression is a serious threat. We all, as a country, need to support them now, for as long as it takes.

We all rallied and stood behind them after 9/11.

We all supported our congressional delegates who voted unanimously to declare War on Terrorism and voted to send our military servicemen and women to war. We can't morally forget about them now!

Soldiers do not pick wars. They do not hope for, start, or declare them. They take an oath, train hard, and prepare to go if they are called upon to do so.

Here are some depressing facts.

Since 9/11, in Operation Enduring Freedom

(Afghanistan), Operation Iraqi Freedom (Iraq) and Operation New Dawn (Iraq), there have been **66,935** soldiers diagnosed with Post-Traumatic Stress Disorder. (Dr. Michael Carino, army office of the surgeon general, September 21, 2010. Data Source is the Defense Medical Surveillance System. As published by Hanna Fischer in Congressional Research Service Report for Congress, 7-5700, www.crs.gov RS22452, published September 28, 2010)

There have been **178,876** soldiers diagnosed with a Traumatic Brain Injury. (The Defense and Veterans Brain Injury Center, http://www.dvibic.org/TBI-Numbers.aspx, updated on May 20, 2010. As published by Hanna Fischer in Congressional Research Service Report for Congress, 7-5700, www.crs.gov RS22452, September 28, 2010)

There have been **1,621** Amputations and **5,674** deaths.

(Hanna Fischer in Congressional Research Service Report for Congress, 7-5700, www.crs.gov RS22452, September 28, 2010)

All these injuries and statistics show a lot of people who are suffering from and are prone to depression. They all need our help, understanding, and unified support for as long as they require it.

For as long as it takes!

Yes, depression *will* find you. Unfortunately, it is true. It is just one of many hurdles that you will have to figure out how to jump over as you progress down your recovery road.

For the severely wounded, it is a hurdle that, more than likely, may have to be jumped over many times while traveling down recovery road.

The depression monster might follow you for years to come as you strive to figure out the new you. But hopefully, with each bout or encounter with it, you will become stronger, and each bout with depression will become shorter.

The depression monster is strong. However, it is *not* invincible. It can be conquered. You can defeat it!

Have faith in the higher power you believe in; have faith in God.

Believe in yourself! In time you will figure things out and find a purpose in life and in things to do that will make you feel productive again and bring you happiness.

Trust in those taking care of you. They want the very best for you. They want you to be the best you can possibly become!

Don't shut out those that love you. Grab on to those who want to reach out and help comfort and care for you.

Don't suppress feelings or thoughts. Talk to someone . . . . anyone that you are comfortable with. But don't try to hide them, ignore them, or keep them bottled up. Doing that is like feeding the depression monster, making it stronger. Share your thoughts and feelings with someone. Lighten your load of mental baggage. There is no shortage of people who are willing to help carry it. There are health care professionals and telephone hotlines, which you can call twenty-four hours a day, seven days a week, and talk to someone, anonymously if you prefer. Your family, friends, veterans' organizations, other veterans, chaplains, priests, reverends, bishops, any religious leader that you have faith in—there is not a shortage of people who are willing to help and listen. Let them in. Let them help you. Why fight depression alone when there are so many that want to help you defeat the monster?

It won't be easy. It is a hard and difficult road you are traveling. However, you do not have to travel it alone.

The war after the war does not have an end date for many.

However, happiness is out there. It is possible for you to have, to enjoy, and to fill your life with it. It is out there for you to grab on to and not only fill your life with but pass on to others and help them as well.

Never give up! Never give in! Don't let depression win the war after the war! Together we can all win.

Believe in yourself.

I believe in you!

G.LEWELL

Danger Mines
PTSD can be like a minefield in your head.

Chapter Eight

Combat-Related Post-Traumatic Stress Disorder (PTSD)

What is PTSD?

Everyone has probably heard of it. But what is it? You were performing your military duty in a theater of war, in combat. Without a doubt, you were exposed to high levels of stress. Just being in a war zone is stressful enough. Now add more stress like, say, a direct encounter with the enemy or an enemy instrument of war, like an improvised explosive device (IED), often referred to as a roadside bomb. Just being in a war zone is stressful enough, no doubt about it. Now throw in bullets flying, bombs, rockets, and mortars exploding; do you think your stress level is going to go up? You're darn right it is. Now throw in poor visibility from darkness, smoke, fire, dust, or blowing sand to add a level of confusion to the situation you are in. More stress, right? Now have all the bullets, rockets, rocket-propelled grenades—have them all aimed at you, have them flying over your head and exploding all around you. Even more stress! You have the knowledge that you are a target for death. The enemy is trying to kill you. That's right, kill you! An element of fear—more stress. Look to the left of you and watch a bullet penetrate the face of one of your brothers, whom you were just joking around with ten or twelve hours ago, and watch as the bullet blows the back of his head off!

Watch brain matter being blown all over! Not enough stress yet?

Fire your weapon back at the terrorist that just exposed himself to shoot at you again. Pull your trigger first and watch your bullets rip through his face and chest. Watch him fall knowing beyond a shadow of a doubt you just killed him. Not enough stress? Look to your right and see the vehicle that was blown up by a roadside bomb burning. Hear the screams from another close friend who is trapped inside and being burned alive. More stress! Keep shooting your weapon at the enemy to try to suppress them while others are trying to pull his body out of the burning vehicle. Look again and see another of the vehicle's occupants screaming as a medic is applying a tourniquet above the knee where a leg used to be.

Not enough stress?

Not enough trauma yet?

Look at the grenade near your feet. Damn, how long has that been there? Turn to drop to the ground and . . . damn, too late. It blows up. Things are now deafly quiet. You are thrown ten meters through the air. Now on your back, you try to get up. The pain is unbearable. You try to scream for help, but no words come. You try to get up but . . . wait, what is going on? You can't get up; you can't move. What the hell? What is this? Where are your legs? That grenade that just exploded blew your legs clear off! Gone!

Pain, oh Lord, the unbearable pain! Where the hell are your legs? "Medic!" you scream. And scream and scream . . . Perhaps it is the last thing you remember.

So what is PTSD? It stands for post-traumatic stress disorder.

According to *Wikipedia*, this is the definition of PTSD:

> Post-traumatic stress disorder (PTSD) is a severe anxiety disorder that can develop after exposure to any events that result in psychological trauma. This

event may involve the threat of death to oneself or to someone else, or to one's own or someone else's physical, sexual, or psychological integrity, overwhelming the individual's ability to cope. As an effect of psychological trauma, PTSD is less frequent and more enduring than the more commonly seen acute stress response. Diagnostic symptoms for PTSD include re-experiencing the original trauma(s) through flashbacks or nightmares, avoidance of stimuli associated with the trauma, and increased arousal—such as difficulty falling or staying asleep, anger, and hyper-vigilance.

Below is a definition of PTSD that is a little more user-friendly, compliments of www.medicine.net:

> Post-traumatic stress disorder (PTSD) is an emotional illness that develops as a result of a terribly frightening, life-threatening, or otherwise highly unsafe experience.

> PTSD sufferers re-experience the traumatic event or events in some way, tend to avoid places, people, or other things that remind them of the event (avoidance), and are exquisitely sensitive to normal life experiences (hyper-arousal).

Another very good source for information about PTSD is www.healmyptsd.com/education/what-is-PTSD.com.

The website listed above is the source of this definition:

> **Combat PTSD:** Combat PTSD denotes post-traumatic stress symptoms resulting from experience in a theater of war.

PTSD has been known by various names, including its American Civil War nickname when combat veterans were referred to as suffering from soldier's heart. In World War I, symptoms that were generally consistent with PTSD were referred to as combat fatigue. Soldiers who developed such symptoms in World War II were said to be suffering from gross stress reaction. Suffering Korean War veterans were said to have been shell shocked, and many who fought in Vietnam were labeled as having post-Vietnam syndrome. PTSD has also been called battle fatigue and shell shock.

The *Diagnostic and Statistical Manual of Mental Disorders, Fourth Edition* (DSM-IV) is the bible for clinical and counseling professionals in psychology and related fields.

Psychiatric diagnoses are categorized by the *Diagnostic and Statistical Manual of Mental Disorders, Fourth Edition*.

Better known as the *DSM-IV*, the manual is published by the American Psychiatric Association and covers all mental health disorders for both children and adults. It also lists known causes of these disorders, statistics in terms of gender, age at onset, and prognosis as well as some research concerning the optimal treatment approaches.

According to the following well-respected website, www. healmyptsd.com/education/what-is-PTSD.com, the following list of general symptoms (provided by Sidran Institute as per the *DSM-IV*) is the official list of what PTSD looks like.

If you recognize yourself in this list, or if you recognize the reflection of someone you love, it's time to get some professional help.

The journey to healing begins with recognizing the problem. Here it is, plain and simple:

In the immediate aftermath of trauma—say, the first month or so—many people suffer from *acute stress*, which includes the following symptoms:

- Anxiety

- Behavioral disturbances

- Dissociation

- Hyper-arousal

- Avoidance of memories related to the trauma

- Flashbacks

- Nightmares

All of these symptoms are part of the normal steps of how trauma survivors process the recent event.

However, if these symptoms persist for more than one month (and begin to functionally and socially impair—and significantly upset—the survivor), then the diagnosis is changed to:

Post-Traumatic Stress Disorder.

- **A.** The person has been exposed to a traumatic event in which both of the following were present:

    1. the person experienced, witnessed, or was confronted with an event or events that involved actual or threatened death or serious injury, or a threat to the physical integrity of self or others

2. the person's response involved intense fear, helplessness, or horror

B. The traumatic event is persistently re-experienced in one (or more) of the following ways:

1. recurrent and intrusive distressing recollections of the event, including images, thoughts, or perceptions

2. recurrent distressing dreams of the event

3. acting or feeling as if the traumatic event were recurring (includes a sense of reliving the experience, illusions, hallucinations, and dissociative flashback episodes, including those that occur on awakening or when intoxicated)

4. intense psychological distress at exposure to internal or external cues that symbolize or resemble an aspect of the traumatic event

5. physiological reactivity on exposure to internal or external cues that symbolize or resemble an aspect of the traumatic event

C. Persistent avoidance of stimuli associated with the trauma and numbing of general responsiveness (not present before the trauma), as indicated by three (or more) of the following:

1. efforts to avoid thoughts, feelings, or conversations associated with the trauma

2. efforts to avoid activities, places, or people that arouse recollections of the trauma

3. inability to recall an important aspect of the trauma

4. markedly diminished interest or participation in significant activities

5. feeling of detachment or estrangement from others

6. restricted range of affect (e.g., unable to have loving feelings)

7. sense of a foreshortened future (e.g., does not expect to have a career, marriage, children, or a normal life span)

D. Persistent symptoms of increased arousal (not present before the trauma), as indicated by two (or more) of the following:

1. difficulty falling or staying asleep

2. irritability or outbursts of anger

3. difficulty concentrating

4. hyper vigilance

5. exaggerated startle response

E. Duration of the disturbance (symptoms in Criteria B, C, and D) is more than 1 month.

F. The disturbance causes clinically significant distress or impairment in social, occupational, or other important areas of functioning.

The above symptoms apply to all types of PTSD.

However, with further classifications come added delineations:

Complex-PTSD:

The first requirement for this diagnosis is that the individual experienced a prolonged period (months to years) of total control by another.

The other criteria are symptoms that tend to result from chronic victimization.

Those symptoms include:

A. Alterations in emotional regulation: This may include symptoms such as persistent sadness, suicidal thoughts, explosive anger, or inhibited anger

B. Alterations in consciousness: This includes things such as forgetting traumatic events, reliving traumatic events, or having episodes in which one feels detached from one's mental processes or body

C. Changes in self-perception: This may include a sense of helplessness, shame, guilt, stigma, and a sense of being completely different than other human beings

D. Alterations in the perception of the perpetrator: For example; attributing total power to the perpetrator or becoming preoccupied with the relationship to the perpetrator, including a preoccupation with revenge.

E. Alterations in relations with others: Variations in personal relations including isolation, distrust, or a repeated search for a rescuer

F. <u>Changes in one's system of meanings</u>: This may include a loss of sustaining faith or a sense of hopelessness and despair

Combat PTSD:

Following deployment in a war zone, many veterans return home significantly altered.

They have a changed view of themselves and the world around them.

For some, reactions to their experiences may be short-lived (perhaps lasting the first few months of reintegration back into civilian life).

For others, healing may require long-term vigilance and care (lasting months, years and even decades).

Typical symptoms of **Combat-Related PTSD** are:

- Survivor guilt

- Cynicism

- Frustration

- Fear

- Negative self-image

- Problems with intimacy

- Distrust

- Loneliness

- Suicidal feelings

- Preoccupation with thoughts of the enemy

- Revenge fantasies

- Addiction

- Alcoholism

- Thinking that feelings are meaningless

- Feeling powerless or hopeless

- Resignation ("don't care")

Regarding the list of typical symptoms of combat PTSD above, I have personally experienced every one of them with the exception of alcoholism, and to be quite honest, I have many times wished I had a bottle of Kentucky Bourbon in the house. I would have taken the top off and thrown it away. I would not have needed it because I would not have had to put it back on. I would not have stopped until I was passed out, the bottle was empty, or I was dead. Sometimes the pain is so great and the emotional feelings and memories so overwhelming that you just want to find a way to escape from them. Just for a moment. You want the memories, the images, and the hurt to go away just for enough time to let you breathe. It is real, and it sucks!

For some time, after I got home, in the morning, my kids would be getting ready for school (three of them were teenage girls). I would still be up from fighting my own war demons all night. The next thing that would happen is they would open the pantry to get some cereal out for breakfast before leaving. They would open the door and find me passed out inside the pantry. Other mornings, they would go sit at the kitchen table and kick something as they tried to slide their chair up to the table. What they would hit was me, passed out under the kitchen table in the fetal position.

Sometimes they would go leave the house and find me passed out leaning against the door of the house. Every time, it was emotional for them. They would have to go get their mom to move me so they could get something to eat or leave to catch the bus.

Of course, this was not only hard for them, but embarrassing and hard for me too.

When being told of the incidents or upon waking when stirred, I would also be embarrassed, ashamed, and hurt. I could not understand what was happening to me. All I knew was I didn't want to be like this. I didn't want to be this guy!

When I got blown up in my vehicle in Iraq, a giant fireball of extreme heat, fire, and gasses engulfed the vehicle, roll over it, so to say. Everyone inside that had any hair exposed, often lost it—eyebrows, eyelashes, mustaches, hair on your hands or arms, whatever. The smell of burning hair is a smell you never forget. The sense of smell is one of the quickest ways to trigger a memory of a PTSD traumatic event. Without knowing it, every morning, girls being girls did what every girl did getting ready for school. They turn on and use curling irons, flat irons, hair crimpers, and blow-dryers. What would come from it was the smell of burning hair, something they were used to and wouldn't even notice. However, for me, the smell would launch me into an abyss that was so overwhelming from the flood of horrid memories and images that would enter my mind. I would shut right down, collapse, try to hide, or pass out. One time, I was even found in the crawl space below my house.

I never had any recollection of anything I was doing prior to being awakened and helped to bed. It was that intense.

Eventually, thanks to my PTSD counselor, Dr. Tom Mullin, he identified the burning-hair trigger, and we were able to counterattack it by the use of simple air fresheners, fragrant candles, and scented-oil warmers strategically placed throughout the house.

Sometimes, finding something to alleviate the symptoms of combat-related PTSD can be that simple. However, no matter how simple, it often takes someone else to recognize and figure that out, the person suffering—in this case me—is too wrapped up in the post-traumatic moment to have an awareness of what is going on around them.

That is one example of why getting professional help is so important. It is not a matter of being weak that you need help. It is simply a matter of you not being mentally aware enough when you are in the middle of a traumatic flashback or traumatic moment to be able to recognize a trigger, even one as simple as a smell that could be diffused by the use of a simple air freshener.

This is also an example of why attending group therapies is also important. Many PTSD triggers are shared by many military members. By attending group therapy sessions and relating this experience, I might have helped someone else who was struggling with a similar PTSD symptom or stressor.

By the same token, by attending group therapy sessions and listening to others relate their own experiences and solutions they may have found to some of their triggers, I may pick up on something that can help me with some of mine. By *not* attending, just think, you may not only be missing out on helping yourself, you may also be missing an opportunity to help one of our brothers or sisters get the help they are searching for by what *you* have to offer the group.

We leave no one behind, remember!

Combat PTSD statistics

- Lifetime occurrence (prevalence) in combat veterans is 10-30%.

- In the past year alone the number of diagnosed cases in the military jumped 50%-and that's just diagnosed cases.

- Studies estimate that 1 in every 5 military personnel returning from Iraq and Afghanistan has PTSD.

- 20% of the soldiers who've been deployed in the past 6 years have PTSD. That's over 300,000.

- 17% of combat troops are women; 71% of female military personnel develop PTSD due to sexual assault within the ranks.   (www.healmyptsd.com/education/what-is-PTSD.com)

Doing the breakdown by war

- Afghanistan = 6-11% returning vets have PTSD

- Iraq = 12-20% returning vets have PTSD (www.healmyptsd.com/education/what-is-PTSD.com)

More PTSD statistics

There has been a Total of **66,935** Diagnosed Cases of PTSD among *Deployed Soldiers* since The war on terrorism, from year 2000 thru September 21, 2010.

Counting *Deployed* and *Non-Deployed Soldiers*; that number combined is over **88,710 Soldiers with PTSD.**

(Hanna Fischer in Congressional Research Service Report for Congress, 7-5700, www.crs.gov, RS22452, September 28, 2010).

Having PTSD is not your fault and does not mean you are weak in any sense of the word. It means you were injured. That is right! You did your duty; you answered the call. You were asked to go to war, and you courageously went without asking questions or trying to dodge the call. You went to war and did everything that was asked of you and more. You survived the harshest of conditions and did so while at the same time in battle with an enemy that was doing everything in their power to *kill* you.

You did so for the love of freedom, your family, friends and your country.

While you were there, you endured, lived through, and survived some traumatic experiences.

Only a very small group of the population has ever experienced the trauma of actual combat. An even smaller group can even imagine the trauma associated with combat. Fewer still could have endured and survived that what you already have.

You went to war and got injured! You were injured physically or mentally; probably both and you survived! Don't forget that. You are a survivor! You literally walked thru hell and survived. However, you are still in a war. Now is not the time to stop fighting. You still have battles that need to be won.

Now you are home, and you are injured. Do not let stupid *labels* keep you from getting the help you need.

Combat PTSD—if you think you have it, by God, go get some help! If not for yourself (because you are too hardheaded), do it for those that love you. Do it for those who have to be around you and put up with you. Do it because you *deserve* to be happy. Don't look at PTSD as a *disorder*. You have an injury from being in combat. If you are hurting, go get the help you need.

All of your injuries need to be treated, not just the ones that are bleeding. Often the injuries that a person cannot see are more serious and life threatening than an open wound that you can physically see. Just like a wound that you can see, if you do not get it treated, it can become infected. Bottling up or trying to suppress symptoms of combat PTSD is like getting an infection in a physical wound. The wound will become harder to treat and left untreated can quickly spread to a serious and life threatening situation that can impact everyone.

If you have a PTSD injury, get it treated. Get the help that you need to treat your injury and keep it from getting infected. The sooner you start getting treatment for your PTSD injury, like any other physical injury, the better your chances are for recovery. I could care less how the Psychiatric Association wants to label your injury. To hell with them! You were injured at war. There is no disgrace in that—none at all! Remember that.

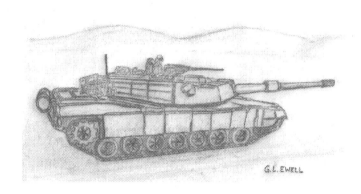

M1A1 Abrams battle tank.

Chapter Nine

Fight for Everything

You are in a war zone and, perhaps, have been for some time. It may even be a second or third tour. For many, even more. You have trained hard. You know your job and your duties well. You have cross-trained and can perform the duties of others, both senior and junior to you, the duties of everyone on your team or squad. You know the duties of everyone on your patrol, in your vehicle—tank, helicopter, boat, ship, or plane. You are skilled and confident. You have seen action before more than likely. You have been engaged with the enemy before. You know what to expect and where danger areas are. You have been briefed on your mission. Pre-execution drills have been performed, and your pre-combat checks have been done. Just as they have been before. Today is just another day at war. Monday, Wednesday—it doesn't matter. A holiday? Who cares? It is just another day. It is a day that will only end when your mission is complete. You wear a watch only to ensure you are on track with times you are to be at objectives or checkpoints. There is no reason to wear one to know when work begins and ends as there is no such thing as a nine-to-five job or regular hours. There is really no such thing as a day off. Everything revolves around missions. Missions evolve around what your enemy is or isn't doing. They often change as quickly as they are received. You know this too well. You hurry up and then wait.

You adapt and overcome. You do what you have to do; you sacrifice and endure.

Yes, just another day. You expect it to be no different than the one before. And then, in the blink of an eye, all hell breaks loose, and your world is forever changed. Perhaps you were on patrol and a fire fight erupted. Perhaps you were caught in an ambush and wounded. Maybe during a predawn assault, the bullet from an enemy machine gun ripped its way through you. You could have been sweeping a house or building and a grenade was tossed into a room you were in. The shrapnel from a rocket, mortar round, or a rocket-propelled grenade tore your body up. Your vehicle could have been blown up by an improvised explosive device (IED) or an explosive formed projectile (EFP). No matter how it happened, it happened. You got shot or got the shit blown out of you. You lost an arm or leg, maybe both. You may have been trapped in your vehicle while it was on fire; then, so were you!

Now you find yourself a casualty of war. Now, you know pain like no other. Instantly, you fight for your very life; you fight for every breath. You may still be fighting the enemy while fighting for your life. Time stands still now. Seconds feel like minutes; minutes, like hours. Hell just became ablaze like never before. You fight to stay conscious. You worry about the other soldiers you are with, your buddies and friends. You still fight for each breath, for your very life. You have been severely wounded. This day is the day the war you were fighting ends. This day is the day your new war begins. This is the start date of your war after the war.

You don't know it yet, but this war will not have an end date. You are severely wounded, and in this war, you will fight personal battles and demons every day for the rest of your life.

A battle buddy may be the first to get to you to get you out of imminent danger and perhaps the first to provide aid to you. Perhaps a trained Combat Lifesaver is quickly at your side. If you are lucky, a combat medic or a navy corpsman quickly tends to you. The whole time, if conscious, you fight for every breath. You fight for your very life. Even if unconscious, I believe something inside you is subconsciously fighting for your life.

Next you are either transported by ground, if you are close enough, or evacuated by helicopter to a US Army Combat Hospital at a forward operating base (FOB). There, doctors, nurses, and technicians work feverishly to stabilize you. Being severely wounded, they know time is your enemy now. They perform miracles to get you ready for the next phase of your journey—a flight to Germany.

From Afghanistan or Iraq, the severely wounded are transported via military transport cargo planes, like the C-17 Globemaster and the C-130 Hercules, which have been retrofitted with specialized medical equipment, to the nearest level 2 military treatment facility (MTC). The closest one is the Landstuhl Regional Medical Center in Germany. It is a seven-hour flight from Afghanistan; from Iraq, it is a five-hour flight.

If you are not in a medically induced coma by now, you may remember the flight as being cold and swear you would freeze to death before you got to Germany.

Yet you continue to fight for your life.

The planes land at Ramstein Air Force Base. From there, the wounded are taken, in specialized busses, to the Landstuhl level 2 military treatment facility (MTF). Their stay at Landstuhl is short, usually about three days to three weeks, just long enough to stabilize them for their next flight—back to the United States.

In the most severe cases, some of the severely wounded are flown directly back to the United States. For instance, a severely burned soldier may be flown directly to the Brooke Army Medical Center in San Antonio, Texas, which is the Defense Department's only burn center (also the army's only level 1 polytrauma hospital). It is a flight that, from the time the soldier is wounded and arrives in San Antonio, can be made miraculously in as little as thirty-five hours (including the stop in Landstuhl, Germany). The wounded are transported via ambulance from the airport in San Antonio to the Brooke Army Medical Center.

Other wounded warriors may be sent to the Walter Reed National Military Medical Center in Bethesda, Maryland (formerly known as the National Naval Medical Center or referred to as the Bethesda Naval Hospital).

Severely wounded service members may end up being treated at a level 1 polytrauma veterans' hospital. Currently, in the Veterans Administration Healthcare System (VAHCS), there are four polytrauma centers in the United States. They are located in Richmond, Virginia; Tampa, Florida; Minneapolis, Minnesota; and in Palo Alto, California.

Level 1 polytrauma centers are considered the most advanced hospitals for veterans and returning-service members. Polytrauma care is for those with injuries to more than one physical region or organ system, one of which may be life-threatening and which results in physical, cognitive, psychological, or psychosocial impairments and functional disability. Some examples of polytrauma include the following:

- Traumatic brain injury (TBI)

- Hearing loss

- Amputations

- Fractures

- Burns

- Visual impairment

You are sent to a polytrauma hospital when there are multiple serious injuries being dealt with at the same time.

Once at the polytrauma hospital, you are assigned a polytrauma team that works with you throughout your stay. The team is tailored to your specific needs, depending on your injuries.

In my own case, I was treated at the level 1 polytrauma unit at the VA hospital in Palo Alto, California.

In Iraq, in 2006, vehicles I was traveling in were blown up by roadside bombs (six different times in fact). I had many issues to be dealt with. My polytrauma team was made up of nine different specialties. I had a primary care doctor, neurophysiologist, speech pathologist, physical therapist, occupational therapist, low-vision specialist, physiologist, a clinical social worker, and nutritionist.

In addition, I saw an audiologist in the main hospital for my hearing loss. I also became one of fifty service members from the war on terrorism that was being seen in the main hospital by the chief of ophthalmology, Doctor John Cockerham, as part of a congressional study titled "Visual and Ocular Damage in Blast Induced Traumatic Brain Injury (TBI)."

My low-vision specialist, Paul Koons, was the first to identify a condition I had, due to my TBI, that he referred to as left-side neglect, wherein my brain would not identify sensory input it received as to what was happening on the left of my body. For instance, I could walk out of a store and stop to look for cars. I would look right and see no cars were coming. My brain would tell me that there were no cars on the left of me. In reality, there were cars coming, and I would never even move my head to look left. The car drivers, thinking I had stopped to wait for them, would continue to drive—about the same time I would decide it was clear and start to walk. I would step right in front of the cars and get run over. This has happened to me many times. I am still trying to find a failsafe technique I can remember to do (which has been the hard part) to keep me safe and prevent this from happening.

This is just one example of the multiple polytrauma injuries I have to deal with and compensate for every single day.

It is hard. It is just one challenge, which is compounded by the many other things that are broken with me. Together, all my problems create a huge challenge that makes every day a fight to get through. Some days are easier than others, but every day is a fight.

My battles will be lifelong. Every day will present challenges and obstacles for my combat wounded and disabled body and mind to get through. Every day, a conscious decision will have to be made: to fight or give in. I choose to fight! Don't get me wrong; there are days that I get tired, frustrated, angry, and depressed and do not feel like fighting. I hate that everything has to be a fight. It is mentally and physically exhausting.

However, I know that in order to have a life full of more happiness than pain, fight I must.

It is said that time heals all wounds. I am not naïve enough to believe that! Nor do I believe it is a statement of fact that will be true for you. We will battle this war after the war, which we (the severely wounded) are now fighting, for the rest of our lives!

This war will not have an end date. I take that back. It will have an end date. That date will be listed on our death certificates. Yes, we will battle with our severe injuries and handicaps every day for the rest of our lives.

Chapter Ten

Lean on Me

Each and every one of us severely wounded at war or who suffered a traumatic event will have a specific time in which we are more prone to, or at a higher risk of, having memories or flashbacks, if you will, to the event. More than likely, there were many events, not just one.

Just as a motorist who was involved in a serious car accident at an intersection may have a hard time driving through that same intersection after the accident or may totally try to avoid the intersection altogether, even if it means traveling miles out of their way to avoid it, you too may try to avoid situations that could remind you of your own traumatic event. You may not even be aware of things that you do, mannerisms you display, or actions you take to avoid a situation, activity, or event that would bring in a rush of horrific or painful memories into your mind. But others will notice. When they do, hopefully, they have enough trust in you that they will let you know about it. If they do, feel blessed and listen to them. When, or if, they do tell you, you need to listen to them. They will tell you because they care about you. They will tell you only if they have trust in you that you will believe in what they are saying. They will tell you because they love you and want to help you overcome some of your abnormal behavior. By knowing these things, you can overcome them. However, if you get upset and yell or scream at them or be in denial and tell them you don't believe what they are saying, they will shut down. They will have their feelings hurt. You have called them a liar and, in doing so, cut off the source of important information and feedback that could be of great help and benefit to you. If you bite back at them when they relate things to you, even if it is things you do not like to hear, they will stop telling you things for fear of getting bitten again. As hard as it may seem, and even though you may believe that no one could understand, you need to have the strength to open a door and let people in. They may not be able to understand what you are going through and feeling. They may not be able to comprehend in detail the magnitude of your traumatic experiences or memories. However, they probably will have enough experience from dealing with their own life's traumatic experiences, sorrow, pain, and suffering that they will be able to share empathy with you.

Hot is hot. A person does not need to stand in the desert in Iraq to know what 120-degree heat feels like. There are places all over America where it gets over 100 degrees, even 120 degrees. And really, once you get over a certain degree, heat is just one thing: miserable. A few more degrees really make no difference at all; it is just miserable.

I was in Iraq just days short of a full year. I know extreme heat. However, the truth is, 113 degrees didn't feel any different than 125 degrees. It was all just miserable heat. Everyone can relate to that. Everyone can relate to pain—it hurts! Pain is pain. Hot is hot. People can relate better than we give them credit for.

So don't shut them out. Let them in, and give them a chance to help.

Especially those you love and that love you. Especially those you love, who are at your side and are there to support you.

Remember one more thing: they have lost something too in *you*! They too are hurting. They too are trying to adjust and deal with how their life has become changed and affected because of what has happened to you. They too are searching for answers and have fears and questions about what the future holds. They too, just like you, are an emotional train wreck on a roller coaster of emotions, with many emotional highs and lows, experiencing ups and downs right alongside you.

Don't shut them out! Those you love and who love you will need to shed many tears. Those you love and who love you will also be in need of someone to talk to and be in need of a shoulder to cry on and someone to hold them.

Somehow, find the strength to be that someone.

While it will be overwhelming and will take the majority of your focus just to hold yourself together and may require the majority of your strength just to focus on dealing with your own pain, demons, suffering, and healing, somehow, if you can save enough energy to be able to let those you love and care about know that you can provide that shoulder for them to cry on, it will make healing together easier. It will greatly improve your odds of getting through your trauma together.

Find a way to let them know that you know those you love are also hurting, scared, grieving, and in pain.

If somehow you could find a way to let them know that you are still strong enough for them, to be able to say, "Lean on me," it opens up the door for dialogue and a release of emotions that could promote an atmosphere in which you and those you love and care about could heal together.

There will come a time when traveling down your recovery road after you have somewhat stabilized and recovered as much as you possibly can, that your recovery road will turn into a journey. A journey in which you will spend the rest of your life learning how to adapt to, deal with, and overcome situations of all kinds as you encounter each of them with your new handicaps. Some people would refer to it as dealing within your new physical and mental limitations. However, I personally hate those terms because I do not see limitations or handicaps. Just circumstances we find ourselves in that we must be more creative in expressing ourselves and dealing with how we interact with the routine of our day-to-day lives.

There will be others along the way that will cross paths with you, both on your recovery road and on your journey. They will want to help out and make things easier for you and your family in a variety of different ways. Some will be individuals just wanting to make a small difference in any way they can. They will want to help just as a way to say thank you for enduring and sacrificing all you have for freedom, for their freedom. Others will be larger groups or organizations.

However, the message will be the same. They simply want to say, "Thank you!"

They will want to say thank you to you and your loved ones for protecting the freedoms that we all enjoy. When those times come, graciously accept what they have to offer you. To turn them down would just hurt their feelings, and that would just be the wrong thing to do. People would not sincerely offer their help if they did not want to. Don't deprive them of the blessings of feeling good that come from doing acts of kindness. Do not deprive you or your family from assistance that could make things easier for all of you.

Whatever you do, don't be pigheaded and look down upon others offering to help as merely providing handouts.

What people and organizations offer you is, as they will tell you, not a handout, but rather, a hand up.

Reach out and take it. Do not be afraid to accept the kindness and gratitude of others. It is not a sign of weakness but strength. Do not be unwilling to let others provide you a shoulder when needed, a hand when needed, a reprieve from the world of doctors, physical therapies, and the continual hard work of healing when offered. Graciously accept, enjoy, love, and laugh in those moments, for they are too short-lived. There will be a time when you will get an opportunity to pay it forward. For now, be thankful and accept it.

Believe me, whether you think you need it or not, each offer, no matter how large or small, will be a big help.

Each offer is merely an outpouring of love in appreciation for what you bravely and courageously stepped forward to do and for what you ended up enduring, sacrificing, and giving up of yourself while there, in a theater of war, doing it.

Do not be afraid to lean on others. Do not be afraid to lean on me.

Someday, I may need to lean upon you.

GLEWELL.

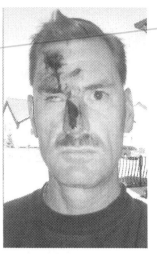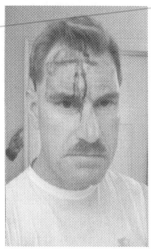

I black out quite a bit. I call it getting unplugged. I don't count a fall unless my head wounds require more than ten stitches to close them. To date, I have had fifty-nine falls that have required ten or more stitches in my face.

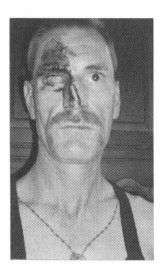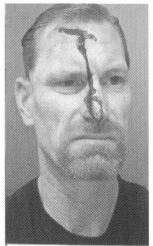

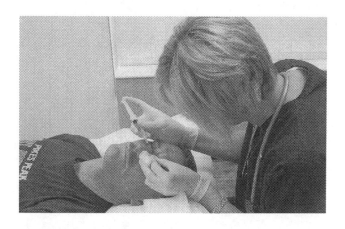

Above and below. Getting some more stitches in my face, a side effect of my brain injury that seems to happen about every six to eight weeks.

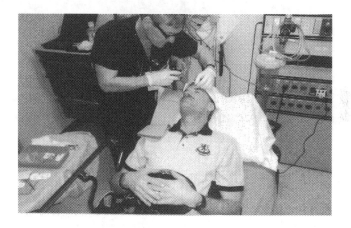

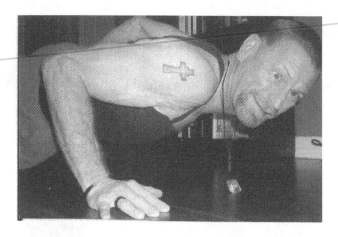

Above: Trying to get stronger by doing one-handed push-ups. I love my dog tags.

Above: Having lunch with dear friends Todd Christensen (*left*), two-time NFL Super Bowl champion (XV and XVIII), and Jerry Bishop (*center*), defender of freedom and Vietnam veteran. After four years of being on a straight liquid diet of five cans of vanilla Ensure every day, I am finally able to eat solid food again.

SECTION TWO

Poems and Poetry of the
Combat Soldier

Congressional Medal of Honor recipient Salvadore
Guintera, a humble and true American hero!

A Day from Hell

A day from hell
The Twin Towers fell
The horror at the Pentagon
And in Pennsylvania a plane of heroes gone

A cowardly terrorist attack
Like a knife stuck in your back
So much bloodshed
So many loved ones now dead

The entire nation did unite
The president sent our military to fight
As Congress gathered and declared war
So this could not happen again upon our shores

As the sun goes down on the East Coast and West
Our citizens all can peacefully rest
Knowing our soldiers now provide a wall
Between us and the enemies that hate us all
Without fear of our country being under attack
Knowing our soldiers are hunting evil men down
Those who brought terror into our cities and towns

Our military deployed with speed
To foreign lands where terrorists breed
To Afghanistan and then Iraq
It is from where they planned their deadly attacks

A Day from Hell (Cont.)

For a decade we have fought long and hard
And kept the terrorist in their own backyard
At home we have enjoyed a decade of peace
And paid for it with bloodshed in the Middle East
The cost has been high, not just with our soldiers' lives
Wounded warriors are now scarred permanently
All selfishly gave so we could be free

So many now suffer from wounds and war injuries
So many, so young, are now amputees
And from the hell the eyes can't see
The crippling wound we refer to as PTSD

Our soldiers stood bravely up to each task
They never wavered and did all that we asked
Now it is time for us to give back
To ensure they are cared for, that not a single one
Slips through the cracks

We owe it to them, each one stood tall
Their own blood they spilled in the sand
So we could enjoy life with no fear at all
While they fought for us in those damned foreign lands

A day from hell, the Twin Towers fell
A terrorist attack like a knife in the back
So many lives lost, so much bloodshed
It is time to bring our soldiers back home
Osama bin Laden, the head of the monster, is dead

I May Take a Life Tonight

I may take a life tonight
I have taken one before
For when a soldier is deployed to war
Someone is dying that's for sure

I may take a life tonight
Killing is not a game
It weighs heavy on one's mind
When it happens, you are never quite the same

I may take a life tonight
I've thought about it long and hard
I have been a soldier all my life
Killing is what I've been trained for

I may take a life tonight
Many battles before I have won
I have been the victor in many fights
Most before the rising sun

I may take a life tonight
Once again out on patrol
For there is evil everywhere
So I get ready, I lock and load

I may take a life tonight
These monsters, they must die
I hate the killing that they do
I face them all the time

I May Take a Life Tonight (Cont.)

I may take a life tonight
I am sick and tired of this fight
It seems that it will never end
My heart can no longer take the pain inside
It will never have time to mend

I pray that I will change my mind
I do not really want to die
Yet I think about it all the time
After every fight
And if I said I wished to live
Well that would be a lie
I tire of fighting evil each and every night

You see where I am on patrol
Is in my very home
And within my very head
As from room to room I roam
Imagine and you too might choose death instead

The life that I may take tonight
Would be my very own
I can no longer fight these demons
And these memories of war
This battle has raged on too long
My heart just cannot take it anymore

I may take a life tonight
I hear Death's footsteps at my door
Dawn is just two hours away
If I can make it, I will live one more day for sure

I May Take a Life Tonight (Cont.)

I will have survived another PTSD battle in my home
Where each night my demons all come out to play
And think that they can freely terrorize and roam
If two more hours can be won, night will turn to day

I will have won another battle
I will have survived PTSD to live another day
And my life will not be lost tonight
Rather the grim reaper sent along his way

Baghdad, Iraq, 2006.

Just Another Day

Today is just another day for me
As I walk through this sand, fly over it, or am at the
ready in the nearby sea
I am a soldier, sailor, airman, or marine
A defender of freedom and damned proud to be

This day is not special nor was the one before
They are all the same for a soldier at war
There is nothing special about it, not for me
Just another mission, and I must succeed

My thoughts will travel to loved ones at home
To those I would call if I could get to a phone
For those I love, I will say a silent prayer today
Ask an angel to deliver them my love, I will pray
And also to protect my squad as we go along our way

There it is as we move out
Just as it was the day before
The sign my eyes don't visualize
It is in my head, this sign is born
It may not hang upon a post I see
That doesn't mean it's not a grim reality

It reads the name of where we are headed
To do the things a soldier must do at war
It makes the reaper's job too easy
For souls are delivered right up to his door
For the sign, it reads, "Valley of the Shadow of Death"
Just like it did the day before

<u>Just Another Day (Cont.)</u>

You see this is just another day for me
The hell through which I travel a constant reality
Though the terrain features, towns, and battles change
The stench of death, the rage, fatigue, and fight
The desire to see another dawn
Is just the same as days that have passed
So I do what I must to keep me and my men alive
Then together we can keep marching on
To a medley of sand flies, scorpions, thirst, and heat
That just adds to the already intense challenges of war

I will sweat and will battle, get fatigued and may bleed
But I will not waver or give up, for I will succeed
A nation is counting on me to be free
For my country and family I will be all I can be
There is no other option at war for a soldier I can see

I Wait and Smoke

I am alone
I light my smoke
My room is dark
So feels my heart
By myself, so all alone
Except for the demons
All sharing my home

I take a drag
Softly my cigar glows
I find comfort as the smoke
Trails by my nose
Another drag, another glow
I quietly wait for them to show
The demons here
All sharing my home

It is almost time for them to come
I will wait I will not run
I will battle them until the break of day
I will survive until I see the light of dawn
Then it will be them that run away
I will still be here, but they will be gone

Soft light as my cigar glows
Again smoke rolls gently by my nose
The smoke is sweet that I inhale
As I sit and wait for my visitors from hell

I Wait and Smoke (Cont.)

I hate that they get inside my head
I cannot shut them out
Horrors of the ugliness of war
That I pack about
Friends that I saw wounded
Friends I now see dead

The time has come
I hear them now
All coming down the hall
I hate that I am all alone
To face them all on my own
But only I can figure how
To make each single demon fall

They are very close
I feel their chill upon the air
I recognize their signals
My body tells me to beware
The time for battle now is near
I will stand tall
I will face them all
Without showing any fear
I won't give them satisfaction
Of showing any tears
At least not during the bitter fight
That will consume every hour
Left until the morning light
Then the tears may come
So will God's bright, warm healing sun

Holiday Opposites

While we enjoy this holiday
A soldier guards a post today
While we laugh as children look wide-eyed at gifts from
Santa's sleigh
A soldier looks wide-eyed for bombs as he travels along
a dangerous roadway

While we enjoy being surrounded by those we love so very dear
A soldier silently sends a prayer for those a world away
That he cannot be with on this holiday
And performs his duties while holding back a tear

Today a soldier somewhere tries to stay warm while in
the frigid cold
While we enjoy carols and listen to Christmas stories being told
Another soldier a world away is in baking heat,
performing his mission today
So we can be comfortable in our homes on this holiday

When all the presents under the tree are gone
We will enjoy a holiday meal with fixings galore
A soldier's day will be hard and long
As they fight to endure another day at war

We will eat until we need a nap
A soldier will wonder when a chance might come to get
some sleep
As they dig for something to eat from their rucksack
We will enjoy second helpings and Christmas treats

Holiday Opposites (Cont.)

From morning until night, we will laugh and play
Most will not have a thought of soldiers in harm's way
Making it possible for us to enjoy in peace the holiday
Yet most soldiers will pray that we all have a merry day
As they do their duties, execute their missions, and go
Along their way

The War after the War

When I was severely wounded in combat in Iraq
At that moment one war ended and another war begun
The war with Iraq is now done
Yet I fight battles daily
Which usually begin with the setting sun

An Improvised Explosive Device "blew-up" my vehicle
In the blink of an eye my world came undone
A split second is all it took
To take away many of my abilities
And Forty-two years of the life I had spun

Now legally blind and deaf
Missing an eye and working ears
Unable to walk without support
Often in a wheelchair is not fun

But the loss of being able to drive at all
Being "Homebound" is the hardest battle right now
I can no longer freely wander around
My precious country I fought so hard to protect
To keep safe and sound

My lungs were damaged by the heat
And gasses of the bombs
Just simply breathing can be a battle at times
As respiratory problems sometimes slow me down

I cannot urinate on my own
I use a catheter to empty my bladder now you see
Because of neurological damage I suffered
From a severe Traumatic Brain Injury

The War after the War (Cont.)

My brain injury left me with memory problems
They create daily battles for me
I can no longer do math or multi-task anymore you see
It takes all I can muster
To focus on just one task at a time now
This is very frustrating for me

These are just some of the problems
That creates daily battles for me to fight
Battles I will be challenged with
Every day for the rest of my life
For the damage is an irreversible, permanent disability

A lifetime of daily battles
Definitely makes up a war
That began when I became a severely wounded in Iraq
That is why I refer to it as the "War after the War"

There are thousands of us fighting battles daily
Challenged with missing arms or legs
Severely burned and suffering
From post-traumatic stress disorders
Related to our combat tour of duty in general
The suffering is not limited to physical injuries you see

The "War after the War" will never end
Not for most of us
Not until a date is stamped on our death certificate
This is very saddening to me
The "War after the War" is much more difficult to me
Than the actual war was in Iraq, I really do believe

<u>The War after the War (Cont.)</u>

None of the severely wounded wants your pity
None of us want to be treated differently
But what I would ask of America is just to be conscious
Of the thousands of severely wounded just like me
Who are still giving and sacrificing for freedoms
That so many take for granted unfortunately

Yes there are thousands of severely wounded
From "sea to shining sea"
They fought gallantry for our precious country
They fought for freedom, love of family and liberty

They now suffer silently
As the country has all but forgot about them you see
Yet they must continue fighting battles daily
In their "War after the War"
I would simply ask that you remember them
And what they are bravely suffering for

Thoughts before Battle
by Richard Hamilton

While I lie darkly in the pit of night
Alert for what grim fate might be in store,
I seem to hear an avalanche of sound
And then, I hear no more;
Till softly, like a vast advancing host
To find me in the darkness where I lie,
A million peepers as in boyhood days
Arrive to sing their old sweet lullaby.

Upon my shoulders where the straps cut deep
To etch their patterns of dull pain,
I feel the gentle touch of something warm,
And very kind, like rain;
Then joyfully she laughs with lips of rose
To kiss my wild and unbelieving eyes,
To whisper life and home and kids
And fill with song the menaced skies.

One hour to go before the great barrage
Will cut the heavens with a sword of flame,
Yet strange that I should dream askance
Of nothing but my own forgotten name,

To see it as I carved it long ago
On that great oak upon the hill,
And feel the bark's strong fingers hold me,
Hug me, want me, love me still!

Soldier's Return
by Richard Hamilton

When the last red tank has grumbled
Through the fortress of the foe
I shall return, my dear,
Full of the vast accumulated love
That from my silent longing
In the southern isles I gathered
As a future gift for you

What desolation passed before my eyes
I counted but a dream
That history in her fetid torment
Passes on to man;
I know that from my faith in you
New cities will be born
Where they dug graves for hostages

Though soil may bitter grow from all
That youthful flesh and blood,
I doubt not that our love
Shall bring a harvest to the world
That will efface the ruins of war,
With grain and joy in such abundance
That all men shall once again be free

So wait, my dear, until my task
Is done, the last attack repulsed,
My bayonet in sheath;
Wait till the earth reconquered rise
To bring me on its shoulders
Back to you, while crowds in glee
Yell loud and wild in victory

<u>Soldier's Return (Cont.)</u>

America awaits you from your battle cry,
The streets and valleys that you love, the faces
That will look so good in Kansas and L.A.
America salutes you, not with martial bands,
But with the silent, grateful heart
The gentle smile, the long prayer
Of giving thanks,; for you shall be the heroes
Who lit candles in the frantic blackout
Of her vast, pulsating, democratic soul
In this dim hour before the dawn America
Prays for you: Oh God, our cause is just,
Our honor firm, our conscience clear
To us belongs the victory!

In Your Honor
by Richard Hamilton

Unselfishly, you left your fathers and your mothers
You left behind your sisters and your brothers
Leaving your beloved children and wives
You put on hold, your dreams—your lives

On foreign soil, you found yourself planted
To fight for those whose freedom you granted
Without your sacrifice, their cause would be lost
But you carried onward, no matter the cost

Many horrors you had endured and seen
Many faces had haunted your dreams
You cheered as your enemies littered the ground
You cried as your brothers fell all around

When it was over, you all came back home
Some were left with memories to face all alone
Some found themselves in the company of friends
As their crosses cast shadows across the land

Those who survived were forever scarred
Emotionally, physically, permanently marred
Those who did not now sleep eternally
'Neath the ground they've given their lives to keep free

In Your Honor (Cont.)

With a hand upon my heart
I feel pride and respect;, my reverence revealed
As tears now stream down my upturned face
As our flag waves above you, in her glory and grace
Freedom was the gift that you unselfishly gave
Pain and death was the price that you ultimately paid

Every day I give my utmost admiration
To those who have fought to defend
Our Great Nation

Friends
by Richard Hamilton

There are days when
bubbling from us comes
the innocent child within,
who giggles at the little things
and wears a silly grin

There are days when
melancholy comes to
visit for a while;
the mind feels tired, the body weak;
we have no strength to smile

There are days when
joy abundant
grabs a hold of you and me;
wraps us up in all its splendor,
lifts us up and sets us free

There are days when
sorrow wraps us
in its cloak of grief and fear,
'til our hearts ache to the breaking,
'til our eyes can't shed a tear

There are days when
love bestows us
with its wonderment and light;
with its beauty and its mystery,
its power and its might

Friends (Cont.)

And there are days when
life rewards us
and seems to make amends
by granting us a marvelous gift,
the precious gift of Friends

Wolf Hamilton and I, visiting veterans at the VA hospital in Martinez, California.

Portrait of a Friend
by Richard Hamilton

I can't give solutions to all of life's problems, doubts, or fears.
But I can listen to you, and together we will search for answers.

I can't change your past with all its heartache and pain, or the
future with its untold stories.
But I can be there now when you need me to care.

I can't keep your feet from stumbling.
I can only offer my hand that you may grasp it and not fall.

Your joys, triumphs, successes, and happiness are not mine; Yet,
I can share in your laughter.

Your decisions in life are not mine to make, or to judge;
I can only support you, encourage you, and help you when you
ask.

I can't prevent you from falling away from friendship, from your
values, from me. I can only pray for you, talk to you and wait for
you.

I can't give you boundaries which I have determined for you. But
I can give you the room to change, room to grow, room to be
yourself.

I can't keep your heart from breaking and hurting,
But I can cry with you and help you pick up the pieces and put
them back in place.
I can't tell you who you are. I can only love you and be your
friend.

Gordy-isms are random thoughts and quotes by me. All are original. They began as I told myself every morning that I had to try to write down something positive, even on days I hurt like hell.

SECTION THREE

Gordy-isms

On a chilly, brisk morning, good friends are like a warm cup of coffee nestled gently between your hands.

—Gordon L. Ewell

You don't have to count true friends using your fingers . . . Their names are already etched on the walls in your heart!

True love is found not where bodies physically collide, but rather where hearts and souls entwine.

Sometimes, in the darkest of nights, the light of love can be found shining brightest from the eyes of a dear friend sent to light your path.

"What goes around comes around"—usually a saying associated in a negative light or as a saying of revenge. However, just think what a wonderful saying and thing it would be if "What goes around" *started* with *love*!

That life can sometimes be a circus is true. However, within each of us is the ability to determine whether we are going to be lion tamers or the clown with the big sad face.

I wish kindness was a secret. Then everyone would pass it on to at least one other person.

Love—if it is not unconditional, you have mistaken it for something else.

You can tell if your heart is in the right place by the occasional blister on your hands from helping others.

When you give from the heart, you don't look for a mention of it in the headlines of the newspaper. You'll feel your headline in the warmth of your soul and the peace in your mind.

Wouldn't it be something if people tried to get as close to their god in times of happiness and joy as they do in times of despair, crisis, and death?

One of the best gifts for any occasion cannot be bought. It is found with humility in the heart contained within a big hug, presented with the sincere smile of dear friendship, and given verbally by simply looking happily into the eyes of the receiver and saying, "I love you!"

The heart of a loved one may be a great distance away with your eyes open, but close them, and you can almost feel their heart beat next to you.

Of all our senses—touch, taste, smell, sight, sound, and some refer to a sixth sense of subconscious or supernatural awareness—I believe the one that often fails people the most is what I call our seventh sense: *common sense*!

Tears are the Miracle-Gro that nourishes flowers of the heart.

Whenever you are getting ready to travel, no matter where, how far, or for what, if the first thing you decide to pack is a positive attitude, you are bound to have a successful journey!

Some say if it is meant to be, it will be . . . I say if you want it bad enough, get off your butt and make it happen! Lack of determination, initiative, and imagination is the only thing that can kill the dreams of a person with freedom.

When crossing fast-moving streams that often run through the path of life we are traveling, good friends are like the solid stepping-stones that will hold you up and allow you to cross the stream without getting your feet wet.

When your world seems to be weighing heaviest upon your shoulders, a dear friend can always find a way to fill your world with helium.

If your heart is in the right place, you may not be able to hear it beat, but someone else will—loud and clear!

LOVE = Listening Openheartedly Very Essential

Kindness is so special it was designed to be able to be delivered in many different packages: a warm smile, a gentle touch, a friendly wink of an eye, a kind word, a soft-spoken voice, the wave of a hand, a kiss . . . No matter how you package and deliver it, kindness will always be well received.

There is but one thing greater than America and the people blessed to live here . . . and that is the Almighty God responsible for the creation of both!

A good visit with old friends is a good reminder of what is truly important in life. It is not titles or what you own. It is love and how you choose to share it with others. No matter how much real time passes between visits, when reunited, you pick up conversations and talk as if you had just seen each other the day before. What a wonderful thing!

We live in the greatest country in the world, not because we have better ideas, imaginations, aspirations, or hopes and dreams than other people in the world do but rather, because we have the fertile fields of freedom in our country to plant those seeds in. God bless America!

If you are determined to see things begin and end with love, the filling in between can be nothing but wonderful.

Jump in your car, and no matter how fast you drive, there are three things you can never outrun: your past, a lie, and the police radio telling the patrol car up ahead how fast you were clocked driving through the speed trap.

I think blessings are like a soft, gentle rain falling down from above. They fall lightly upon us and all around us every day. Too often, people are so busy waiting to witness a miracle in tsunami proportions that they are blind to constant gentle rain of daily blessings.

Plan for the worst, hope and pray for the best, and count your blessings if things fall somewhere in between.

While cruising down the highway of life, good friends are the suspension on our vehicle. They help absorb the shock of the bumps, potholes, and rocks in the road—which could cause pain and misery—and help make the ride of life as smooth and enjoyable as possible!

Everyone on the planet is handicapped or disabled. Some physically, some mentally, some when it comes to love, some spiritually . . . and others are handicapped without the common sense or humility to *not* make fun of and show compassion toward those who are truly suffering from a handicap or disability!

There is no tapestry in the world more skillfully and carefully woven with ethnicity, heritage, racial tolerance, religious expression, individual emotion, intellectualism, compassion, freedom, and love than the alluring beauty of the tapestry of Americana! Woven within it is a very small but ever-so-strong thread that holds it all tightly together. That thread is called *veterans*!

All things change but one. Time changes, seasons change, and people and things age, and as all do, there remains one constant—God's love. It can be found in all time, in any season, available to all people, and it never dims.

When the road ahead appears to be all uphill, don't get discouraged. Rather, keep reminding yourself of how beautiful and majestic the view will be when you get to the summit.

The reason pets can't talk is because God did not want us to feel constantly embarrassed by how much more common sense they have than we do.

If you like yourself and feel good inside and out and have a peace of mind, you are beautiful. If you can do the things you want without easily tiring, you are healthy. If both of these apply, I don't care what your bathroom scale says. You are beautiful and healthy! When I become dictator, I will outlaw bathroom scales.

Love knocks or calls, often when you least expect it, and quietly and gently comforts you like a warm blanket on a chilly morning. It gives and takes but is not selfish in that it never takes more than it gives, when it is both given and received first from your heart.

Coffee is so good in part to its hidden meaning. Coffee stands for "come over for friendship everyone enjoys!"

Everyone has heard that it is always darkest before the storm. A good time to buy flashlight batteries is on a sunny day. But in case you forget and a storm hits, don't forget there is always a light you can turn on. To access the switch is easy . . . simply take a knee.

If the majority of people would *act* all week long like they do on Sunday, the world would be a wonderfully different place to live in.

The loving and unprejudiced heart can make the right decision long before the uneducated mind that waits without faith for facts.

If you are dead set on judging a book by its cover, make sure it's *your* story that is written on the inside flap.

Blind faith—listen to your heart and strive for things you think are beyond your grasp. Just think, if someone did not stand on a shore staring at the horizon with determination and say, "I know there is something beyond what I can see," we would all still believe the world was flat.

If you don't believe grown men cry, just walk into any bar or club at closing time on a Saturday night and look around when you hear the bartender holler out, "Last call!" You could irrigate five acres of farmland with all the big ol' tears you'll see well up in eyes of every grown man in the place.

Laughter is good medicine. But with all medicines, there are side effects. You may experience sore cheeks from oversized smiles, sore ribs from continuous laughing, or even a rare bladder discharge from uncontrollable laughter. Despite the side effects, it is one medicine I wish everyone could be prescribed with, share their prescriptions, and even have an occasional overdose of.

It is a fact that laughter is good medicine, social interaction keeps the mind active, and getting rid of stress can ward off a heart attack. All these things are provided by a dear friend. Just think of the many health problems you could avoid and help someone else avoid by simply being kind, being a good listener, sharing laughs, and willing to open your heart.

Afterword

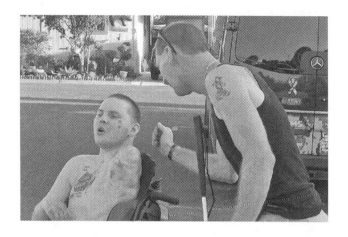

With my brother Jerral Hancock,
Iraq War veteran, Purple Heart recipient.

No one comes back from a war the same man or woman they were before they left. No matter how badly one wants to believe they escaped unscathed, the truth is, every single soldier leaves a war scarred, one way or another, if they are fortunate enough to return at all.

Soldiers know the risks and dangers of their profession. Just as a policeman, fireman, or anyone else in the business of putting themselves in harm's way to protect others know of such dangers and risks of their profession. Yet they courageously step forward and take an oath to protect and defend, knowing there may come a day that they may not live to see another sunrise, family, friends, or home again. They train hard to diminish the odds of that day occurring. But nothing can totally eliminate those odds. In war, it is a fact someone is going to meet their Creator.

It is also a fact that many soldiers will get wounded, some more than others, many severely. Many soldiers will suffer from wounds the eye cannot see; mental wounds like post-traumatic stress disorder (PTSD), for some, can be every bit as disabling as physical wounds.

For the wounded, the date they became a casualty of war may be the date a new war begins, a war of survival in which every single day, for the rest of their life, they will fight a battle just to get through the day and on to the next. A war in which every single day they will have to battle and learn how to adapt to their new world with severe handicaps like missing limbs, sight, or hearing, or brain and neurological malfunctioning.

For the severely wounded soldier, the date they became a casualty of war may be the end date of the current war they were fighting. However, it is just the beginning of a new war, the war after the war, in which they will fight every single day for the rest of their life. They will then, in essence, be fighting a lifetime at war.

This war, unfortunately, will be filled with casualties as well. Families may be torn apart, loved ones lost, or friends abandoned. It will be filled with heartache and pain, both the soldiers' own and of others' who love and care about them. There will be long, grueling periods of intense pain during the recovery and rehabilitation stages following their initial injuries. There will be a lot of pain to follow as they learn to use prosthetic devices. There will be more pain when they return home and learn to adapt to the new world that awaits them with their new handicaps. Some will have chronic pain that will never go away.

Their pain will seem endless at times and, for some, may in fact be. It will come from many sources. There will be both physical and mental pains as well as spiritual pain and heartache. The source of the pain may take some time for doctors and mental health professionals to figure out. Conventional medicines may help some but not all. New, and old, holistic medicinal practices may be able to help some soldiers but not others. One must keep an open mind and be willing to try different things while under their doctor's supervision to find the safest long-term pain management plan for them. It could be a combination of both that works best.

During this time, frustration, hopelessness, fear, and anger may become serious issues that will need to be dealt with as well. For the severely wounded, time is an enemy because it does take a long time during this phase of the recovery road to stay focused on continuing to heal and progress in a positive light when one is hurting so badly. It is during this time that relationships are so volatile and prone to destruction. This is also a time that a soldier typically is at a greater risk of falling into the hands of addictive behaviors like drug abuse and alcoholism. It is during this time that the emotions of frustration, hopelessness, and depression open their door the widest to try to let suicidal thoughts wander into one's mind and make them believe that it is the only way out.

I know this from the literally hundreds of wounded warriors I have spoken to over the last six years, and listening to them tell me when these feelings hit them the hardest. I know this from living through it myself and knowing when these feelings were most dominant and overwhelming for me. It is a difficult time at best to get through. Knowing and accepting that this new you will dominate the remainder of your life is tough. It is difficult to embrace, and it takes time to rediscover you. It takes time to get to know, accept, and love you. Yes, parts of the old you remain intact and are noticeable. But the wounded warrior you now are is dominant and has qualities and attributes that are more dominant, which others will probably notice before you do yourself.

That you are wounded is not something negative. That you have changed does not mean at all for worse.

In fact, some changes may have brought out better qualities or made old ones even stronger than they were prior to becoming severely wounded.

But the fact remains, there have been characteristic physical and mental changes in you that are different, which you need to reconnect with. To do so is often best done under the care—or coaching, if you will—of a mental health professional and by attending some individual and group therapy sessions. Not because you have a disorder or an illness but, rather, simply because it is easier to accomplish knowing you are not alone. It is easier to accomplish knowing that what you are feeling and facing, others are feeling and facing as well. Do not forget, you may hold the keys or have a thought or comment that someone else is waiting to hear to get over a hump in their own recovery road.

Do not forget we are a team. We look out for each other. We leave no one behind, remember?

Do not forget that you are not the only one that has to adjust, accept, and get reacquainted with the new you. Your spouse, children, family, and friends need some time to get reacquainted with the new you as well. It may take them a little time too. Give them that time. Allow it to happen, and it will. Don't forget that what makes you who you are and what makes you special comes from within you! It is not the shell that houses or encompasses you. People fell in love with you for *who* you are, not because you had five fingers and toes, or because you were six feet three inches tall. Do not forget that. That element of you is still within you. It always will be!

To my severely wounded brothers and sisters, don't ever give up. Keep fighting the good fight! Never say never, never say die! You can get through this. You can endure, and things will get better. You will figure it out and reconnect with yourself and others. If you want it, happiness is waiting for you. It is out there; it is yours to be and to enjoy. It is what you enlisted for and took an oath to protect and defend. You did just that and paid a heavy price doing it. But you did it. Now fight for, go after, follow, catch, and enjoy what you preserved—the American dream!

Whether you are a wounded warrior or the caregiver of a wounded soldier, it is my sincere desire that if you are troubled, do not be afraid or ashamed to ask for help. If you know someone who you think is suffering, do not be afraid to intervene, either directly or indirectly. A phone call could save a life. Above all, know that help is out there. *Help is available!* Please do not let yourself, or someone you know suffer, and go without.

Until this realization comes, so many needing help will never get it. Until this realization comes, how this harsh reality will continue to manifest itself will be in the continued increasing statistics of domestic violence, drug and alcohol abuse, divorce, suicide, and severe depression among the ranks of such a special group of Americans—the American soldier.

Less than 2 percent of our entire population is serving in our armed services, willing to shoulder the burden of defending our freedoms whenever and wherever called upon.

We as a nation owe it to these people to ensure they are taken care of. Not just to take care of physical wounds but mental scars of war as well.

We as a nation owe it to the families of these warriors to take care of the families as well. They too are suffering. They too have scars and trauma from war. Their lives have also been adversely affected. Many are now in the unasked roles of lifelong caregivers for their soldier, and they need to be taken care of, to be trained, and to receive benefits for taking on the role and not running from it.

Our wounded warriors, active military servicemen and women, and our veterans and their families deserve our gratitude, our appreciation, and our support.

Our severely wounded deserve to be taken care of. No matter what their needs, no matter what it takes.

No matter how long it takes!

God bless them all, each and every one.

May God bless America and forever keep her the land of the free and the home of the brave!

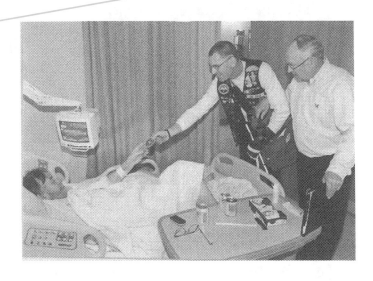

Visiting hospitalized veterans with
Command Sergeant Major Dell Smith (retired).

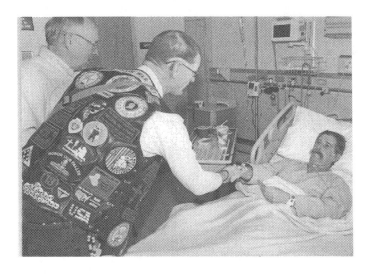

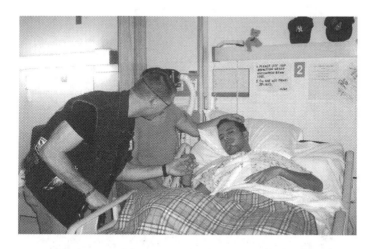

Above and below: Visiting hospitalized veterans.

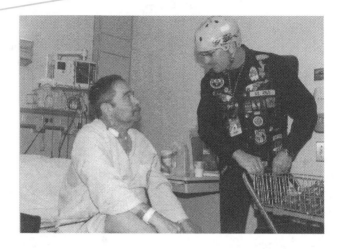

Above and below. Visiting hospitalized veterans.

Prayer for the Wounded

Dear God in Heaven above
I reach out to you this night
For my family that needs to feel your love
They need your help to stand up and fight

It is my brothers and sisters you see
Some were severely wounded during the war
They got hurt real bad physically and mentally
And need your strength now for all they must endure

The night will bring demons to their door
Their days will be long and painful too
Some of them Lord, they just can't take no more
All the surgeries and therapy can really make them blue

But I was sure that you could help the see
Beyond these present days and nights of hell
That currently consumes them constantly
And leaves them without the strength to even yell

It's hard for them to believe that others know their pain
And that they want to help them, in any way they can
To get thru the darkness that surrounds them all in vain
To thank them for protecting our freedom in this land

Reach out to them Lord and ease their pain
Give them the strength to understand
That it will not forever rain
And let them know it is okay to accept a helping hand
For this I humbly ask thee Lord, in your son's holy name

Signing my first book, *Dung in My Foxhole*, at the University of Southern California during the Los Angeles Times 2012 Festival of Books.

About the Author

Master Sergeant (MSG) Gordon L. Ewell was born on June 8, 1967, and graduated from Emery County High School in May 1985. He joined the Utah Army National Guard on August 28, 1985, with initial assignment to the 1457th Engineer Battalion as a combat engineer. In August 1991, he transitioned to the Active Guard Reserve program with Delta Company of the 1457th Engineer Battalion.

His twenty-four-year career has been marked with distinction through notable accomplishments that render him an excellent example for other soldiers to follow.

Throughout his outstanding military career, he has served in key positions as training and administration specialist, supply sergeant, combat engineer squad leader, and personnel section sergeant.

From Master Sergeant (MSG) Gordon L. Ewell's initial entry into military service, his superiors recognized his outstanding initiative and a deep care for his fellow soldiers. He has been recognized as one who would do whatever it takes to accomplish the mission or help a fellow soldier in need. MSG Ewell has graduated from over thirty army resident schools, graduating as the honor graduate, or in the top 10 percent of his class, from nearly every one of them.

He completed, with a superior rating, over one thousand hours of army correspondence training. Additionally, he earned an associate degree in science in April of 1999.

During his service in Iraq, MSG Ewell performed fifty-nine challenging and dangerous missions, which involved both the coordination of convoy route route clearance and route clearance observation missions, based upon his knowledge and expertise in these areas. MSG Ewell was vital in the creation of the first route clearance handbook and was further recognized by the corps staff as the multinational corps subject matter expert in route clearance. His lessons learned in Iraq have been published in many army periodicals.

MSG Ewell led over 33 percent of the missions he was on in Iraq. He was recognized by his superiors to be unparalleled in his physical stamina and toughness, complemented with superior technical and tactical capabilities. This was clearly demonstrated on the battlefield when his efforts under heavy enemy fire were unrivaled, which earned him a Bronze Star Medal, the Purple Heart Medal, and the Combat Action Badge.

During his combat missions, on six separate occasions, a vehicle he was in was blown up by improvised explosive devices (IEDs). One of the explosions was so powerful that it blew impacted wisdom teeth out the side of his jaw. In addition to major jaw damage, he suffered from broken vertebrae in his neck, damage to his lower spine, and permanent loss of his hearing.

He suffered the anatomical loss of his right eye and peripheral/bilateral vision loss in his left eye, leaving him legally blind. He has a traumatic brain injury (TBI), flaccid neurologic bladder, loss of balance, an abnormal gait, and he is fighting to overcome post-traumatic stress disorder (PTSD).

MSG Ewell returned from combat duty on December 2006 and was assigned to the 640th Regiment, Regional Training Institute. Because of the severity of his combat injuries, he was medically retired due to injuries sustained while at war in February 2010.

His medical journey to date includes six major surgeries and treatment at eight different hospitals in three different states by over forty-seven different doctors, surgeons, specialists, and other health care professionals, not counting more than a dozen different dentists, endodontists, oral surgeons, and other dental specialists.

Today, though he is 100 percent disabled, he continues to serve with distinction as a member of the Blue Star Riders and is a volunteer at the George E. Wahlen VA Hospital in Salt Lake City, the Veterans of Foreign Wars, the Disabled American Veterans, and the American Legion.

The retired master sergeant currently resides in Eagle Mountain, Utah. He enjoys being a father and watching his babies grow.

He also enjoys public speaking, writing, helping other veterans, and the beach.

Military Awards and Decorations

Bronze Star Medal
Purple Heart Medal
Meritorious Service Medal
Army Commendation Medal (with Bronze Oak Leaf)
Army Achievement Medal
Army Good Conduct Medal (with six Bronze Knots)
Army Reserve Components Achievement Medal (with three Bronze Oak Leafs)
National Defense Service Medal (with Bronze Star)
Iraq Campaign Medal (with Campaign Star)
Global War on Terrorism Service Medal
Armed Forces Reserve Medal (with "M" Device and Silver Hourglass)
NCO Professional Development Ribbon (third award)
Army Service Ribbon
Overseas Service Ribbon

Army Reserve Components Overseas Training Ribbon (third award)
Combat Action Badge
Driver and Mechanic Badge (with wheeled vehicle clasp)
Sharpshooter Weapon Marksmanship Badge
Utah Commendation Medal (third award)
Utah 2002 Olympic Winter Games Service Ribbon
Utah Emergency Service Ribbon
Utah Achievement Ribbon
Utah Recruiting Ribbon
Utah Service Ribbon
Joint Meritorious Unit Award
Army Superior Unit Award

Noteworthy Civilian Achievements

City of Eagle Mountain Outstanding Citizenship Award (2007)

The State of Utah Department of Public Safety Executive Award of Merit:

In recognition and appreciation of extraordinary service and outstanding contributions on behalf of the citizens of Utah (2008).

Was one of six people from Utah selected to hand-stitch the Utah section onto the National 9/11 Flag that now resides at the museum at Ground Zero as a national memorial and treasure (July 2011).

Elected as the senior vice commander of his Disabled American Veterans Chapter, Wasatch One, Utah (August 3, 2011).

Was honored to be made an honorary member of Rotary International, with membership in the Park City, Utah Sunrise Club (August 15, 2011).

His most treasured titles and accomplishments are the following:

- Father

- Son

- Brother

- Friend

- Patriot

- Veteran

- Author

- Volunteer

Public speaking.

Speaking to kids in elementary school about patriotism and customs and courtesies to the American flag.

Above: Doing patriotic service announcements with Paul Swenson.

Below: my friend Brett Hutchings, Major (Retired) U.S. Army and owner of Hutch's Fine Home Furnishings.

Acknowledgments

A severely wounded warrior can enjoy a productive life full of hope and success when surrounded by the love of family and the fellowship of friends, in part because of the many volunteers and charitable organizations who truly want to help them.

Suicide is still taking the lives of more of our soldiers than the enemy is. This is not acceptable! I believe we need to invest more time and resources identifying those who need help, those whose silent cries for help continue to go unheard. Help is available. For too many, they simply do not know where to find it. Money should *never* be a factor in determining if a wounded defender of our nation receives the treatment or care that they need.

To everyone who has helped me or my family during my long and ongoing recovery road, I thank you! You know I will never forget your kindness, your care, your bedside manner, your listening ears (to lots of my anger and frustrations) as I have learned to live in my new world or your financial support. I could fill an entire book with the names of people I feel I will always owe a debt of gratitude. From the humble heart of a broken old warrior, I sincerely thank you all!

Special thanks to Paul Swenson (Colonial Flag and the Healing Field Foundation and employees) as well as Brett Hutchings (Hutch's Fine Home Furnishings and his friendly employees). There would not be a book without your help. Thank you for your friendship too!

Rod and Marjory Ewell, my parents.

My two princesses
Scarlett (left) and Lincoln Abbygale (right).

To my princesses, Daddy loves you to the moon and back! You are my Northern Stars as I navigate life.

Mom and Dad, you always show me unconditional love. You still ensure I get where I need to be and what I need and never complain or ask for anything in return. Your sacrifices of both time and money on my behalf are appreciated beyond measure.

My dad spent forty-three months of hell in Vietnam. He received a Bronze Star, Purple Heart, and the Vietnam Cross of Gallantry with thirteen palms for his courage and sacrifices there. My grandpa Ferguson served in the navy, contributing toward the bill of freedom as well.

I met another Vietnam veteran while at the polytrauma unit at the VA hospital in Palo Alto, California—the founder of the Blue Star Riders, a group that visits the wounded in hospitals. He visited me and became a friend a man only gets once in a lifetime. Thank you, Wolf (Marsha too)! You continue to look after our wounded. I enjoyed staying with you this summer!

Command Sergeant Major Dell Smith, another lifetime friend, continues to look out for me. You were always at hand, from Iraq through each stage of my recovery, and you continue to let me be your sidekick. Thank you, my friend (Connie too)!

To my dear friend Dennis Cattel (Vietnam veteran, Army Ranger, friend to all), a man of honor! I miss you dearly. Your days on patrol are over. You rest now among men of honor in a castle of eternal glory!

With Utah governor Gary Herbert,
an honorable man I am proud to call friend.

At a town hall meeting with the Honorable
Congressman Jason Chaffetz and my dear friend
Command Sergeant Major Dell Smith (retired).

Above: With Utah Senior Senator Orrin Hatch

Below: With Utah Senator Mike Lee

Above: With Major General Brian L Tarbet

Below: With Brigadier General Jefferson S Burton

The following organizations make my present and future brighter than I could have ever imagined:

- The Blue Star Riders (Wolf, Marsha, Tony, and Vicky)

- Homes for Our Troops (John Gonzales and staff)

- The Coalition to Salute America's Heroes

- The Eagle Cane Project (Jack Nitz, founder and friend)

- Wounded Warrior Project

- AW2 (Army Wounded Warrior Program)

- Vet-Tix (special thanks to Eddie Rausch)

- Center for Prosthetics Inc. (Carole and Joe)

- Utah Joint Forces Charitable Trust

- Palo Alto Health Care System, Palo Alto, California (Director Freeman; Kerri Childress and staff; ophthalmology chief Dr. G. Cockerham, K. Glynn-Milley, and everyone in Polytrauma; and Scott Skiles)

- The Fisher House Foundation

- George E. Wahlen Veterans Hospital in SLC, Utah (Director Young; Jill Atwood; Dr. West; Dr. P. Miller; Dr. T. Mullin; Dr. Roberts and Polytrauma; Jim Stritikus; Diane, Pam, and "B" and Dental; Belinda Karabatsos and volunteer services; Sharon Jones, Thomas Wolf, and the low-vision staff; Greg, Dan, Maxine, Barbara, and Mike; all my providers, their assistants, and their staff; and my family of volunteers—my friends, I need another book to list you all!)

Above: Jeff Sagers, the most honest man I know.

Below: Wolf Hamilton, the most giving man I know.

A special thank-you to some special people who have helped me wander along my recovery road:

- Melba Wahlen, I love you dearly. Thank you for being such a wonderful friend, just like George.

- Alexandra Eframo, my personal angel, and Arnold.

- Todd Christensen, for caring for veterans and lunches.

- My aunt Marilyn, for all you do and rodeo too.

- Montel Williams, thanks for your example and friendship.

- Richard Evans, Diane too, for letting me run with you.

- Brigadier General Jefferson Burton, *Essayons!*

- Montgomery Gentry, Eddie and Troy, I'm always keeping an eye out for you; I'm honored to call you friends.

- Toby Keith, your support of our troops is second to *none.*

- Kam Wright, for always being there. Thanks for LA.

- Robyn Glade, thanks for patching me up.

- Ernest Chamberlain—Grace, Vesta, and staff—*love!*

- John Crosby (CSM [Ret.], 19th SF, army) "All but 9."

- Red Atwood, is the boat ready?

- Jim Lish, you are still covering my six.

- Kip Day, love ya, brother.

- Ross Low (SGM [Ret.], army) wordsmith and friend.

- P. W. Covington, always in the trenches for veterans!

- Stacy Bare, avid outdoorsman and veterans advocate.

- Blackie and Harold, for taking me under your wings.

- Jerry Bishop, Vietnam veteran, gagon dragon buddy.

- Dave Baker, Vietnam veteran, my friend and light.

- Wade Ewell, quit working on your truck and come see me.

- Dr. Blaine Austin, for making it possible for me to eat!

- Brad Howe, my surf master and dear friend.

- Jay and Metta, for miles of smiles whenever I see you.

- Ann Jensen, for always growing orange sticks.

- John Glines, thanks for always driving me East.

- All my friends in Oscoda, Michigan.

Above: My dear friend Melba "George" Wahlen.

Below: Author Richard Paul Evans, always inspiring!

To all men and women who have worn the uniform of a defender of our country and her freedoms, I commend you! You are part of a very special and elite group of our Americans that currently is less than 4 percent of our nation's total population. That in itself makes all of you heroes in my book!

To *everyone* who supports our country's military servicemen and women, I sincerely thank you! You play a vital role in our nation's security. Without you, they could not do their mission and stay focused if they had to worry about the support of the nation they are called upon to defend.

To those who have endured cold, dark nights in Europe's Black Forests; the cold, bitter bite of a Korean winter; the damp endless rains of Vietnam; the disease and humidity of dense jungles and island hopping throughout the Pacific; the heat of Africa and Somalia; the terrain of Afghanistan; and the blasting sandstorms of Iraq, in battle, I salute you! You have intestinal fortitude, endurance, and courage beyond measure.

To my brothers and sisters, wounded warriors who are suffering mentally or physically, I have empathy for you. I suffer with you. Stay strong and never give up; continue the fight! Look out for one another, and remember that we leave no one behind.

For those who gave all, I will never run out of tears.

Above: Banner of me and friend Robyn Glahe outside the assisted-living facility I lived in.

Below: Red Amy and Troy McCann at the motorcycle ride for charity Brandon's Ride.

Above: with Marjory Ewell, my mother, and Montel Williams.

Below: My brother Wade and friends Eddie Montgomery and Troy Gentry, giving them my book.

Above: Showing Toby Keith a vehicle he signed that I drove in Iraq.

Below: Marine Corps General James Conway.

Above: American patriot and friend Roger Mooney, one of the best rodeo announcers in the USA.

Below: Mike and Anne Collett and Ken Barfield (president) Park City, Utah, Sunrise Rotary Club—an incredible chapter of super volunteers for humanity.

Above: Me Surfing with AmpSuf at Pismo Beach, CA

Below: With my Surf-Master and Friend Brad Howe
(Brad is also a Vietnam Veteran).

Talking to Colonel Gregory Gadson, director of the
Army Wounded Warrior Program (AW2)

Appendix 1

Resource Tips

The key to gaining access quickly to much-needed resources, as well as eliminating as much stress as possible as one navigates the different government bureaucracies and charity organizations, relies on two main factors.

First, have you and/or your service member's vital records handy and readily available? No matter which organization you deal with, or major charity, they will all ask for the same few vital documents or for the information that comes off them. You should put together and have available in one place at least the following documents:

1. **DD Form 214**. You may have more than one. The very last is most important. It shows the service member's dates of service, grade and rank, awards, schooling, total years of service, and type of discharge. You should take a copy to the Department of Veterans Affairs Office near you. They will certify it and keep a file on record; in case you lose yours, you can get a copy from them quickly if you have provided them one.

2. **Orders awarding a Purple Heart**. Not the pretty certificate to hang on your wall but the permanent order that authorized and announced the award of the medal.

3. **Licenses and Certificates**. Marriage license, birth certificates, and death or divorce documents, if it applies.

4. **Two forms of pictured identification**. You should immediately get registered at your nearest VA hospital or outpatient clinic. They can direct you where you need to go to get loaded into the system and get you a veteran's ID card made. Besides being used for VA services, the card is an excellent second form of identification.

5. **Expect long waiting periods**. While getting better, the system is not breaking any sound barriers, so to speak. You *will* have periods of long waits, feel like you are in lines that never move, and could get easily frustrated. Three words will drastically cut down on your frustrations. They are patience, patience, and *patience*! Best I can tell you is, take a book, magazine, or MP3 player with you.

Second, *do not delay getting registered in the VA system*. You may not see urgency now. However, once in the system, you are always in the system. Don't wait until you are in dire straits to get registered, years down the road when important information is forgotten or lost. You can get the ball rolling even if you are still on active duty orders. Don't put it off. Getting registered is vital to your long-term health care needs!

Here is some more food for thought.

Ask a lot of questions, and seek out the help of others who have been there before you. They are willing to help and can save you a lot of time and guesswork.

Also, *every service organization has a service officer* to assist you in filing a claim or providing information. The Veterans of Foreign Wars (VFW), Disabled American Veterans (DAV), Military Order of the Purple Heart (MOPH), American Legion—every one of them has people trained to help you navigate the system.

I would *strongly recommend* joining a service organization, like the VFW, DAV, or American Legion. Go to an occasional meeting. The people already in the system love to share information and can pass along, from experience, things to do or avoid doing, which will drastically cut down on your time by not having to reinvent the wheel, so to speak.

Remember that veterans' facilities are _your_ facilities! You, and only you, can make them stronger and better. Do *not* hesitate to tell someone when you do not get the service you deserve. If you find a problem, try to think of a better way of doing things, a solution to your problem. Fill out a suggestion card. They have suggestion-card boxes everywhere. *It pays to use them!*

Suggestion cards are not just for complaints either. If something or someone is doing a *great* job, let someone know. That way the good things get noticed, reinforced, and become common practice rather than fade away. I can guarantee you the director of the VA hospital or health care system where you are will read every single one of the suggestion cards.

You or your caregiver *must* learn to be your own health care expert. Get the current VA benefit handbook. I cannot reiterate that strongly enough! Ask questions. Keep asking questions if you do not get satisfying answers. *Be persistent!* Remember, they are *your* facilities and benefits. *You earned them!* Get the most from them. Get the *help* you deserve and need.

It is a sad but true fact that there are many programs, entitlements, and grants out there, through the VA, that you will need and will improve your quality of life. However, you will never hear about them unless you are proactive and read all you can about them or hear about them from attending a service organization meeting. No one will be falling all over you to let you know of things you should and need to know are available. For instance, you may be eligible for a Special Adaptive Housing Grant (SAH).

This pays up to $64,000 to remodel your home to make things more accessible and easier for you to get around and take care of yourself. There is a vehicle grant that will pay up to $11,000 for a vehicle to carry your wheelchair. The VA will install a lift in a vehicle to transport the wheelchair. You should get a power chair and a manual wheelchair both. Be sure to inquire. Depending on how far you travel, you should get reimbursed for the mileage you travel to the VA for scheduled treatments. I cannot drive because of my combat injuries and was paying other people to take me to my appointments nearly every single day for over a year before I found out about the travel reimbursement. I could have used that to pay people rather than paying that out of my own pocket. But no one explained that to me. I heard about it at a VFW meeting. They can only go *back* 30 days for payments.

Find out how often they will replace your glasses, how long before you can upgrade your hearing aids, and how often you are entitled to get two sets of hearing aids or two pair of glasses, depending on our disability status. You need not be shy and inquire. If you don't, you could be missing out because, odds are, you won't be told if you are eligible for things like these. Canes and aids to help you get dressed, devices to help in the kitchen, handheld grabbers that help you reach things on high shelves that you cannot reach from your wheelchair. There are forms for you to get free public transportation passes, reduced property taxes, or property tax abatement; free federal national park passes. Your state may offer free fishing and/or hunting permits and state park passes. You can have your prescriptions mailed to you rather than have to go into the hospital pharmacy to pick them up, and much more.

These are just a few examples. My point is, there is no one person to tell you all these things. You truly have to be proactive with your recovery, treatment, and care. One more thing: document *everything!*

Appendix 2

Resource Information

The following pages are a list of *both* government-funded programs as well as charitable organizations that have been set up properly under Federal Code 501-(C)-(3) as nonprofit charities so that your donations to these worthy organizations can be tax deductible. Both offer amazing programs and help for our nation's combat-wounded warriors.

Many grateful patriotic citizens noticed needs that our severely wounded war veterans have. Needs that would not get taken care of because of a lack of government funding if it were not for the hard work, ingenuity, and creative thinking of many thankful citizens and a network of thousands of wonderful volunteers.

If not for the founders of these awesome charitable organizations, grateful American patriots, and both small business and corporate sponsors, there would be thousands of severely wounded soldiers and their families who would be in some pretty dire situations. There would be many severely wounded soldiers and their families who would have a quality of life that would be heartbreaking and unacceptable at best; and few—if any—would ever know part of the American dream, like owning a home or putting children through college A few government programs and private charities are below. They are not listed in any order. These I know of personally or have been helped by, and I testify they do the work of angels daily.

Behavioral Health Resources

National Suicide Prevention Lifeline: With help comes hope! Are you in crisis? Then call 1-800-273-TALK or Chat, right now. If you or someone you know is in an emotional distress or suicidal crisis, please call the Lifeline at 1-800-273-TALK (8255), 24 hours a day, 7 days a week, and 365 days a year. Web: http://www.suicidepreventionlifeline.org/

Phone: 1-800-273-8255 (24/7 Availability)

Military OneSource is a free 24-hour service available to all active duty, Guard, Reserve members and their families regardless of activation status. Information and referrals are given on a wide range of issues including behavioral health. Face-to-face, phone and online counseling services are available.

Web: www.militaryonesource.com
Phone: 1-800-342-9647 (24/7 Availability)

Defense Centers Of Excellence Improving the lives of our nation's service members, families and veterans by advancing excellence in psychological health and traumatic brain injury prevention and care.

Web: http://www.dcoe.health.mil/Default.aspx
Phone: 1-866-966-1020 (24/7 Outreach Program)

Behavioral Health Resources (Cont.)

<u>The Veterans Crisis Line</u> connects Veterans in crisis and their

families and friends, with a qualified, caring, Department of Veterans Affairs responder, through a confidential toll-free hotline, online chat, or text. Call 1-800-273-8255 and Press 1, chat online, or send a text message to 838255 to receive help 24 hours a day, 7 days a week, and 365 days a year.

Web: http://www.veteranscrisisline.net/Default.aspx
Phone: 1-800-273-8255 (24/7 Availability)

<u>Tricare beneficiaries</u>, including retirees and their dependents, are eligible for civilian outpatient mental health treatment.

Standard and Prime patients may receive up to eight visits of outpatient mental health care without authorization. Prime patients must use network providers.

Web: http://www.tricare.mil/mentalhealth/

<u>FOCUS</u> (Families Over Coming Under Stress) provides

resiliency training to military families. It teaches practical skills to meet the challenges of deployment and reintegration, to communicate and solve problems effectively, and to successfully set goals together and create a shared family story.

Web: www.focusproject.org
Email: info@focusproject.org

Top Rated Charity Organizations

Homes for Our Troops, a national non-profit, non-partisan 501(c)(3) organization founded in 2004. We are strongly committed to helping those who have selflessly given to our country and have returned home with serious disabilities and injuries since September 11, 2001. It is our duty and our honor to assist severely injured Veterans and their immediate families by raising donations of money, building materials and professional labor and to coordinate the process of building a home that provides maximum freedom of movement and the ability to live more independently.

The homes provided by Homes for Our Troops are given at NO COST to the Veterans we serve.

Homes for Our Troops
John Gonsalves—Founder
SMA (USA, Ret) Ken Preston—President and Director
Dawn M. Teixeira, Executive Director

Mailing Address:
Homes for Our Troops
6 Main Street
Taunton, MA 02780

Phone: 508-823-3300 or Toll Free: (866) 7 TROOPS
Fax: 508-823-5411
Web: www.homesforourtroops.org

Top-Rated Charity Organizations (Cont.)

<u>The Coalition to Salute America's Heroes</u> <u>(CSAH)</u> was created to provide a way for individuals, corporations, and others to help our severely wounded and disabled Operation Enduring Freedom and Operation Iraqi Freedom veterans and their families rebuild their lives.

The mission of the Coalition to Salute America's Heroes is to assist individuals and their families who have been severely injured while serving in the US military during our country's defense against terrorism and to encourage and assist other organizations and the general public to participate in this effort.

Roger Chapin—president, CEO

CSAH is a 501(c)(3), nonprofit, nonpartisan organization, founded in 2004, and headquartered in Wilton, Connecticut.

Mailing Address:
Coalition to Salute America's Heroes
12 Godfrey Place
Wilton, CT 06897-3030

Phone: 1-(888)-447-2588
E-mail: info@saluteheroes.org

Web: www.saluteheroes.org

Top-Rated Charity Organizations (Cont.)

 **Soldiers' Angels** is a volunteer-led 501(c)(3) nonprofit providing aid and comfort to the men and women of the United States Army, Marines, Navy, Air Force, Coast Guard, and their families. Founded in 2003 by the mother of two American soldiers, its hundreds of thousands of Angel volunteers assist veterans, wounded and deployed personnel and their families in a variety of unique and effective ways.

"May No Soldier Go Unloved," encapsulates the motivation behind Soldiers' Angels. The volunteers of Soldiers' Angels work tirelessly to demonstrate active care and concern for veterans, the wounded, deployed service members and their families.

President/CEO: Patti Patton-Bader
E-mail: pbader@soldiersangels.org

Mailing Address:
Soldiers' Angels
1792 E Washington Blvd
Pasadena, CA 91104

Phone: 626-529-5114
Fax: 626-529-5446
Voice Mail: (615) 676-0239

Web: www.soldiersangels.org

Top-Rated Charity Organizations (Cont.)

SEGS4VETS (DRAFT) *"Mobilizing America's Heroes"* Segs4Vets is an unprecedented grass-roots effort sustained and administered by volunteers representing grateful Americans, who passionately believe that when those serving our nation are sent into harm's way and suffer serious injury and permanent disability they must have every resource and tool available to them, which will allow them to fulfill their dreams and live the highest quality of life possible.

Candidates for the Segs4Vets program have sustained injuries which have resulted in the amputation of one or both legs, extensive soft tissue and muscle injuries, traumatic burn injuries, spinal cord injuries, traumatic brain injury, and other neurological injuries and disorders.

Segs4Vets has been certified as one of the best charities in America, by the Independent Charities of America. *This honor is accorded to fewer than 2,000 of the more than one million public charities in the United States today.*

Segs4Vets/
Disability Rights Advocates for Technology
500 Fox Ridge Road
Saint Louis, Mo. 63131
Phone: 800-401-7940 (office)
Fax: 314-965-4956 (Fax)

Web: www.draft.org

Top-Rated Charity Organizations (Cont.)

 **Blue Star Riders** is a nonprofit organization. We are Mothers, Fathers, Brothers, Sisters and fellow Vets who support those who defend our freedom. We are dedicated to supporting our troops and veterans, as well as honoring all wounded troops and fallen heroes.

Our activities include visiting the wounded and their families at Level 1 Poly Trauma Centers, Hospitals, and Outreach Centers, to let them know they have not been forgotten; providing comfort items as well as personal hygiene products to our hospitalized heroes; attending funerals for fallen heroes, and spreading the word of the Fallen and Wounded Warrior Torch.

Founder & President: Richard "Wolf" Hamilton

Mailing Address:
Blue Star Riders
P.O Box 121
Oakley, CA/ USA
94561

E-mail: info@bluestarriders.com

Web: www.bluestarriders.com

Top-Rated Charity Organizations (Cont.)

*** <u>EAGLE CANE PROJECT</u> ***

Our goal is to provide PRESENTATION CANES to a select group of Post 9-11 Veterans who have received some manner of leg disability from combat related actions.

The Presentation Canes are based upon an eagle head design, personalized for the veteran. When possible and or practical, canes are to be carved and presented by participants from the same state as the veteran.

In January 2004, while watching an ABC News about our wounded post 9/11 Veterans, *I realized that there was, perhaps, a little something that I, a woodcarver and cane maker, could do to indicate to these young people our support and to bring some measure of honor to them.* Since many of the Veterans presented on the ABC segment displayed leg wounds and amputations and would most likely be using a cane at some time, *I thought that we could carve symbolic "Presentation" canes, not as an everyday use object, but as an artistic representation of our support and respect.*—Jack Nitz

If you know of a veteran with leg injuries sustained in post-9/11 service,

Contact Jack Nitz
Phone: 1 (918) 299-2251
E-mail Jack Nitz at: <u>thehickoryhiker@gmail.com</u>
or *Stan Townsend* at: <u>staninvent@cox.net</u>.

Web: www.eaglecane.com

Top-Rated Charity Organizations (Cont.)

 **Ampsurf** is a nonprofit organization made up of amputees, veterans and friends and family of the disabled. We want to Promote, Inspire, Educate, and Rehabilitate people with disabilities. Especially, our Veteran Heroes, through adaptive surfing and fun safe outdoor activities that everyone can participate in and enjoy.

One in five Americans will struggle with a life-long disability. Nearly two million men and women have served our country in Iraq and Afghanistan. They are coming home looking for ways to feel whole again and to fit back in to normal life. Whether they are an amputee, visually impaired, suffer from PTSD (Post-Traumatic Stress Disorder), or have quadriplegia. Whether they served in WWII, Korea, Vietnam, the Gulf war, Iraq or Afghanistan. *AmpSurf offers a unique program to bring the healing power of the ocean and adaptive surfing together for an experience that is both mentally and physically one of the best forms of rehabilitation on the planet!*

Phone: 1-(805)-744-8622

AmpSurf
P.O. Box 5045
San Luis Obispo, CA 93403

Web: www.ampsurf.org

Top-Rated Charity Organizations (Cont.)

VeteranAid.org: Salutes ALL Veterans thru Benefit information and how to apply for it. The Aid and Attendance (A&A) Pension provides benefits for veterans and surviving spouses who require the regular attendance of another person.

The Veterans Administration offers Aid and Attendance as part of an "Improved Pension" Benefit that is largely unknown. This Improved Pension allows for Veterans and surviving spouses who require the regular attendance of another person to assist in eating, bathing, dressing, undressing, medication dosing, or taking care of the needs of nature to receive additional monetary benefits. It also includes individuals who are blind. This important benefit is overlooked by many who need additional monies to care for loved ones.

Aid and Attendance can help pay for care in the home, Nursing Home or Assisted Living facility. A Veteran is eligible for up to $1,704 per month, while a surviving spouse is eligible for up to $1,094 per month. A Veteran with a Spouse is eligible for up to $2,020 per month (based on figures from Dec 2011).

The Improved Pension is not a new benefit, and has in fact been an entitlement for 60 years sitting idle while millions have and still are missing out on.

Web: **www.veteranaid.org**

Top-Rated Charity Organizations (Cont.)

It's in the nature of Military and Veterans to step up. So we did!
The kind of people who volunteer to serve their country, the ones who put their nation first and their own lives second, are the kind of people we need to honor every day. Not just on Memorial Day, Veteran's Day and the Fourth of July, but every day.

Through **The Veteran Tickets Foundation**, now those who care about our Military and Veterans have a way to give back. Every day, in every city, there are events with empty seats that could be filled by those who serve or served. More than that, many event tickets are simply unaffordable for average people. We believe the events that bring Americans together in the spirit of celebration, competition and camaraderie—those all-American moments are the times we need welcome and acknowledge our Veterans.

Mailing Address:
Veteran Tickets Foundation
3401 East Turquoise Ave.
Phoenix, Arizona 85028

FAX: fax your documents to 520-350-9314 (cover sheet required)

Web: www.vettix.org

Top-Rated Charity Organizations (Cont.)

 **<u>Injured Marine Semper Fi Fund</u>** is a 501(c) (3) nonprofit set up to provide immediate financial support for injured and critically ill members of the U.S. Armed Forces and their families. *We direct urgently needed resources to post 9/11 service members from all branches of service—Marines, Navy, Army, Air Force or Coast Guard—as well as their family members.* The Semper Fi Fund (SFF) provides relief for financial needs that arise during hospitalization and recovery as well as assistance for those with perpetuating needs. *Our program provides support in a variety of ways including:* Service Member and Family Support, Specialized & Adaptive Equipment, Adaptive Housing, Adaptive Transportation, Education and Career Transition Assistance, Post-Traumatic Stress Disorder and Traumatic Brain Injury Support and Team Semper Fi.

Injured Marine Semper Fi Fund
Wounded Warrior Center • Bldg. H49
Camp Pendleton, CA 92055
Phone: 760-725-3680 or 760-207-0887
Fax: 760-725-3685

Injured Marine Semper Fi Fund
715 Broadway Street
Quantico, VA 22134
Phone: 703-640-0181

Web: www.semperfifund.org

Military Programs

 **The Warrior Transition Command:**
WTC's mission is to develop, coordinate, and integrate the Army's Warrior Care and Transition Program (WCTP) for wounded, ill, and injured Soldiers, their Families or caregivers to promote success in the force or civilian life. *The establishment of the WTC also represents a milestone in the Army's transformation of outpatient care and services. This began with the* **Army Wounded Warrior Program (AW2)** *and continued with* **Warrior Transition Units (WTUs)** *worldwide*

Warrior Transition Command
200 Stovall Street, 7S27
Alexandria, VA 22332-5000
Phone: (703) 428-7118
Email: warriorcarecommunications@conus.army.mil

Wounded Soldier and Family Hotline
"Staffed 24 hours a day 7 days a week"
Toll Free: (800) 984-8523
Overseas DSN: (312) 421-3700
Stateside DSN: 421-3700
Email: wsfsupport@conus.army.mil

U.S. Army Wounded Warrior Program (AW2)
200 Stovall Street, Suite 7N57
Alexandria, VA 22332-5000
Toll Free: (877) 393-9058
Overseas DSN: (312) 221-9113
Email: AW2@conus.army.mil

Military Programs

The Air Force Wounded Warrior *Care Beyond Duty!* The Air Force will take care of its Wounded Warriors. We will fully support the Office of the Secretary of Defense programs to keep highly skilled men and women on active duty. If this is not feasible, the Air Force will ensure Airmen receive enhanced assistance through the AFW2 program.

Strong emphasis is placed on ensuring wounded Airmen receive professional, individualized guidance and support to help them successfully navigate their way through the complex process of transitioning out of the Air Force and returning to civilian life.

Contact:

AFW2 Program Office
Toll Free: (800) 581-9437
Fax: (210) 565-3385

Mailing Address
HQ AFPC/DPSIA
ATTN: AFW2
550 C St. West, Ste. 37
Randolph AFB, TX
78150-4739

Web: www.woundedwarrior.af.mil.

Military Programs

Navy Safe Harbor Providing Non-medical Care for Seriously Wounded, Ill, and Injured Sailors, Coast Guardsmen, and Their Families *"Numquam Navigare Solus"*—Never to Sail Alone

Navy Safe Harbor is the Navy's organization for coordinating the non-medical care of seriously wounded, ill, and injured Sailors, Coast Guardsmen, and their families. Through proactive leadership, the program provides a lifetime of individually tailored assistance designed to optimize the success of shipmates' recovery, rehabilitation, and reintegration activities. Eligibility: All seriously wounded, ill, and injured Sailors, Coast Guardsmen, and their families:

OEF/OIF/OND casualties
Shipboard accidents
Liberty accidents
Serious illnesses (physical or psychological)
The Navy Safe Harbor provides a lifetime of care.

Contact Us
Navy Safe Harbor's toll-free number, 1-877-746-8563, or email safeharbor@navy.mil.

NAVY PERSONNEL COMMAND
5720 Integrity Drive
Millington TN 38055-0000

Web: http://safeharbor.navylive.dodlive.mil

Government Listings

 American Red Cross **The American Red Cross, Service to the Armed Forces**, Keeping Pace with the Military. The American Red Cross links members of the U.S. Armed Forces with their families during a crisis. Twenty-four hours a day, 365 days a year, the Red Cross quickly sends emergency communications to deployed service members on behalf of their family. Both active duty and community-based military can count on the Red Cross to provide emergency communications that link them with their families back home, access to financial assistance in partnership with the military aid societies, information and referral and assistance to veterans. Red Cross personnel form a global network in 700 U.S. chapters, military installations worldwide and in forward deployed locations in Kuwait, Afghanistan and Iraq.

To Find Your Local Chapter:
Phone: 1 800 RED CROSS (1 800 733 2767)

Contacting National Headquarters:
Phone: (202) 303-5214—Staff / Dept. directory

Mail:
American Red Cross National Headquarters
2025 E Street NW
Washington, DC 20006

Web: www.redcross.org

Government Listings

 The VA Mission Statement: To fulfill President Lincoln's promise *"To care for him who shall have borne the battle, and for his widow, and his orphan"* by serving and honoring the men and women who are America's Veterans.

Visit the VA website for a wealth of information and services, as well as to order your free copy of the current VA Benefits Handbook: www.va.gov

Veterans Services

Veterans of the United States armed forces may be eligible for a broad range of programs and services provided by the VA. Eligibility for most VA benefits is based upon discharge from active military service and certain benefits require service during wartime.

Health Care

VA's health care offers a variety of services, information, and benefits. As the nation's largest integrated health care system, VA operates more than 1,400 sites of care, including hospitals, community clinics, and community living centers, domiciliaries, readjustment counseling centers, and various other facilities.

Phone Number for General Questions:
1-800-827-1000

Web: **www.va.gov**

Government Listings

Military Pathways: Mental Health Screening & Information.

To help those who may be struggling, the Department of Defense teamed up with the nonprofit organization, *Screening for Mental Health*, to launch **Military Pathways** (formerly the *Mental Health Self-Assessment Program*). The program is available online, over the phone, and at special events held at installations worldwide. *It provides free, anonymous mental health and alcohol self-assessments for family members and service personnel in all branches including the National Guard and Reserve.* The self-assessments are a series of questions that, when linked together, help create a picture of how an individual is feeling and whether they could benefit from talking to a health professional.

The primary goals of the program are to reduce stigma, raise awareness about mental health, and connect those in need to available resources. The self-assessments address depression, post-traumatic stress disorder (PTSD), generalized anxiety disorder, alcohol use and bipolar disorder. After an individual completes a self-assessment, s/he is provided with referral information including services provided through the Department of Defense and Veterans Affairs.

Web: **http://militarymentalhealth.org**

Community Healing, Honor, and Pride

Colonial Flag Foundation develops and implements many programs to promote patriotism, a sense of civic duty and honor for those who serve our country. Our programs encourage volunteerism and unity, generate awareness and raise funds for issues in support of civic, service and other nonprofit organizations, and create an environment that helps to heal, honor, celebrate and educate.

COLONIAL FLAG
FOUNDATION
Healing Field & Field of Honor Flag Display Programs

Colonial Flag Foundation was organized in 2003 shortly after the first Healing Field display was orchestrated by *Paul Swenson*, President of Colonial Flag in Sandy, Utah. ***That first event was organized as a way to visualize the sheer enormity of human loss that occurred in the terrorist attacks of September 11, 2001.*** It became a personal gesture of support, a tangible expression of mourning, and a very real healing experience.

Through *Colonial Flag Foundation* communities come together, visitors are educated and uplifted; and *most importantly, individual hearts are healed.*

Colonial Flag Foundation
9362 South 300 West
Sandy, UT 84070

Phone: 801.256.3639
Toll Free: 866.375.3524
info@healingfield.org

Web: http://www.healingfield.org

The following list contains more awesome top charity organizations Just type the name or reference in **bold** into the search engine on your computer to find out more about them.

General and Multiple Assistance

Armed Forces Foundation—Housing renovations, outdoor sports, grants, bereavement support.

Freedom is Not Free—Financial assistance.

Hope for the Warriors—Grants, family housing during recovery, spouse scholarships, family/spouse support, "wishes" for severely wounded.

National Resource Directory—Clearing house for national, state, and local private/government information and resources.

Operation Second Chance—Hospital visits, home renovation, and transition support.

Paralyzed Veterans of America—Help with health care, benefits, and career opportunities.

Rebuild Hope—Financial assistance.

Wounded Warrior Regiment—Full range of support for marine/navy wounded and family.

Wounded Warrior Project—Sports activities, grants, transition/employment, and family adjustment support.

Recovery and Sports

Angels of Mercy—Gifts/visits for the hospitalized.

Azalea Charities Aid for Wounded Soldiers—Gifts for the hospitalized/veterans.

Care Pages—Free patient blogs.

Heroes on the Water (KASA)—Fishing and kayak outings (at major medical centers).

Operation TBI Freedom—Free care-coordination services (advocacy/advice).

Operation Oasis—Therapeutic massage and spa services for wounded and family (San Antonio, Texas).

Texas Honor Ride—Supporting the Soldier and Family Assistance Center at BAMC.

The Mission Continues—Fellowships to empower wounded and disabled veterans to serve in their communities.

Wounded Heroes Foundation—Outings, hospital visits, and care packages.

Families of the Fallen

Patriot Guard Riders—Honor guard and protection for funerals.

Housing and Transportation

Air Compassion for Veterans—Transportation for specialized treatment/rehab.

Fisher House—Housing for family/outpatients at medical facilities.

Rebuilding Together—Home renovation.

Veterans Airlift Command—Private plane transportation for wounded during recovery.

<u>Employment and Advocacy</u>

American Combat Veterans of War—VA advocacy and PTSD support.

America's Heroes at Work—Employment support for veteran with TBI or PTSD (Department of Labor program).

JOFDAV—Job opportunities for Disabled American Veterans

Special Operations Command Care Coalition—Advocacy, information, and transition assistance.

<u>Miscellaneous</u>

Kindle—Christian prayer support.

Appendix 3

Phone Listings

The following is a *phone* contact list of organizations whose primary focus is on crisis and crisis prevention, and help programs for *all* soldiers and their families.

Military One Source

It is a twenty-four hour help by phone. Help with life's "big" and "little" issues. Not a question or topic that cannot be discussed. From physical and mental health concerns, social concerns, fear and anxiety to how to change your car oil or bake a cake. No kidding!
ARMY: 800-464-8107
MARINES: 800-869-0278
NAVY: 800-540-4123
AIR FORCE: 800-707-5784

National Veterans Foundation

(800)777-4443. This is the only nationwide nongovernmental national hotline for veterans and their families. They provide emotional support, crisis intervention, and benefit information. Also see their website at http://www.nvf.org.

Social Security Office Locator

(800)772-1213. Veterans suffering from PTSD may be able to obtain Social Security Benefits even if the VA refuses them.

Phone Listings (Cont.)

National Suicide Prevention Lifeline

1(800)273-925
Note: 9255 spells TALK. (800)-273-TALK.
The *only* National Suicide Intervention hotline funded by the federal government, this number works twenty-four hours a day, seven days a week and has over 100 crisis centers nationwide. Currently suicide is taking the lives of more of our soldiers than the enemy is in Afghanistan. It has to stop. If you think you know someone in need of help, please do not look away. Help is out there! Help is available!

REALifelines

They offer employment assistance for seriously wounded veterans who otherwise could not return to work.
(877)872-5627
(877)US2-JOBS

Less than 4 percent of the American population has served in, or is currently serving, in a branch of our armed services.

The American soldier does not go to war and fight and risk being severely wounded or dying because they hate the people, culture, race, religion, or politics of those they see in front of them. They go to war and fight and give their best because of an unconditional love for all they left behind to protect: family, friends, freedom, our flag, and the American dream!

No matter what your political views are . . .

No matter what your opinion is of war . . .

You can disagree with the politics and with the congress that has to vote and elect to declare war to send soldiers to fight one and still support the American soldier!

Soldiers do not make wars. Nor do they decide when or where to fight one.

Soldiers march when and where they are told to. When they get there, they do what they have been trained to do to the very best of their ability.

Soldiers do not fight for a hatred of what is in front of them. They fight for what is behind them that they love. Things like freedom, love of family, love of country, friends and property. They fight to protect these for everyone in America and to perhaps make it possible for others of humanity to also enjoy.

This is one reason why it has been said that the American soldier is quite possibly the greatest promoter of peace on the face of the planet.

Thank you for supporting our servicemen and women and their families. All gave some. Some are still giving!

Some gave all!

G.L. EWELL

The End